Community, Hierarchy
and Open Education

Community, Hierarchy and Open Education

Gary Easthope
School of Social Studies
University of East Anglia

Routledge & Kegan Paul
London and Boston

First published in 1975
by Routledge & Kegan Paul Ltd
Broadway House, 68-74 Carter Lane,
London EC4V 5EL and
9 Park Street,
Boston, Mass. 02108, USA
Set by Red Lion Setters, Holborn, London
and printed in Great Britain by
Unwin Brothers Limited
© Gary Easthope, 1975
ISBN 0 7100 8210 X (C)
      0 7100 8211 8 (P)

For Chris and Mike

Contents

Chapter 3   The Sovereign Head

Part 2   Hierarchy

Chapter 4   Four Ideologies against Hierarchy

Chapter 5   The Reality of Hierarchy

Contents

Part 3   Open Education

Chapter 6   Open Education

Chapter 7   The Open School

Preface

This short book is meant as a guide to many and complex ideas which are more fully discussed elsewhere, not as a full discussion of those ideas. It looks at the various educational theories in English education at the present time and seeks to relate these theories to empirical evidence about the reality of schools where this is available. Although ideas and evidence are cited from other countries the focus is upon the peculiar English conception of a school. This does not imply that the ideas and evidence cited in the book are not applicable to other parts of the United Kingdom or other countries but only that such application must be moderated by an awareness of the different traditions and practices of those countries.

There is no intention to proscribe or prescribe any particular educational theory but merely to point out the implications of each theory with respect to the empirical evidence and three themes: community,

Community
hierarchy
open education

hierarchy and open education. Each theme can be
interpreted as a discussion of those ideas which, as
Halsey (1972) points out, are the seminal political
ideas of our age: liberty, equality and fraternity.
Educational discussion of the theme of fraternity is
presented in the section dealing with community,
discussion of the theme of equality is presented in
the section entitled hierarchy, and liberty is discussed
in the final section on open education.

Acknowledgments

This book is a succession of debts to friends and colleagues. The original impetus for the book came from my doctorate thesis and for help with that I must thank my supervisors Dr King and Professor Mitchell, Mrs Fry who stopped my wilder flights of research fantasy and taught me that good research depends as much on good letter writing as theoretical ideas, and all the staff of the schools involved who gave me their time and understanding. In addition the research would not have been finally possible without the aid of a small grant from the SSRC.

Fortunately this book is not a revamped version of my thesis. Since writing the thesis I have had the good fortune to discuss my ideas with John Wilkes of the New University of Ulster, who has worked closely with me on Bernstein's ideas and their practical implications, Chris Turner and John Corbin of the University of East Anglia who have forced me to develop my ideas about equality and community

respectively and Adrian Bell, of Keswick Hall College
of Education, who added to my understanding of
Bernstein's thesis on 'open schools'.

I must also express a sincere thanks to the
succession of typists who have struggled to decipher
my writing, particularly Morag Stark who typed the
thesis and Mary Gurteen and Julie Shuttleworth who
typed the book.

My thanks are due to the following for permission
to reproduce copyright material: R.A. King and
Routledge & Kegan Paul for allowing me to adapt a
number of tables from *School Organization and Pupil
Involvement*; Colin Lacey and Manchester University
Press for a table first published in *Hightown
Grammar*; and R. Lambert and the Trustees of the
Social Administration Research Trust for the tables
taken from *New Wine in Old Bottles*.

Part 1

Community

Chapter 1

Three Conceptions of Community

[handwritten margin annotations: Social order / Hobbes / Hierarchical / Rousseau / Contractual / Sense of justice / Communitas / individual paramount]

Society is an invention of individuals for without
individuals there can be no society; the individual is
an invention of society for without society there can
be no individuals. To talk of individuals separate from
their societal context or to talk of society apart from
the individuals of which it is comprised is therefore
to talk nonsense. And yet this tension between the
concepts, the abstract ideas we call the 'individual'
and 'society', underlies debates in philosophy,
education, sociology and many other intellectual
disciplines. It underlies these debates because once
having distinguished the individual from society it
becomes necessary to demonstrate the relationship
between the individual and society, and different
philosophers, educationalists and sociologists have all
produced different descriptions of that relationship
and different prescriptions for what that relationship
should be. It is these different descriptions and
prescriptions that form the theme of this book.

This tension between the individual and society is
presented obliquely as a tension between community
and hierarchy, freedom and order, fluidity and
structure, because by presenting the tension in these
terms rather than directly in terms of the individual
and society insights can be gained into current educational controversies. Amongst educationalists, both
those who theorise about it and those who practise it,
there is at present a war being fought. For purposes of
exposition this war can be seen as a war between two
proponents, with allies on both sides. On the one side
are ranged those who celebrate individuality, freedom,
experiment and openness whilst on the other are
those who stress order, structure and hierarchy. It
is a conflict between those who want to give more
freedom so that men may realise their true potential
as men and those who argue that an ordered society is
essential for men to exist, and that men can only find
their true potential within an ordered society. This
conflict between individual freedom and societal
order underlies the different conceptions of
community held by philosophers, sociologists and
educationalists for different conceptions of
community represent different degrees of emphasis
upon the freedom of the individual. Writings upon
community can be crudely classified into three
categories, although there are works that fit into
more than one category. In the first category are
those sociologists and political philosophers who are
concerned primarily with the maintenance of social
order, and for whom the individual exists to serve
society. This first category may be described by the

term 'hierarchical community'. In the second category are those sociologists and political philosophers who are concerned with the freedom of the individual but see that freedom being exercised within a social order. In this conception society exists to serve the individual. This will be called 'contract community'. The final category has no concern with social order at all. In this conception the individual is paramount and the problem of social order is not one that is faced. This is the conception of community as 'communitas'.

Hierarchical Community

The concept of 'hierarchical community' is expressed most clearly in the work of Hobbes (1962). Starting from the premise that any individual has a fundamental right to protect his own life, Hobbes argues that to achieve this requires men to give up their freedom to a ruler, for if they do not give up their freedom then they will not live as true men because all their time will be occupied in an unending 'war of all against all'. Thus from a premise based upon individuality Hobbes arrives at the conclusion that good order in society must take precedence over any individual. The society conceived of by Hobbes is therefore hierarchical. There is a hierarchy of power with two positions on the hierarchy, that of ruler and ruled. In such a society the individual exists to maintain the society and retains his individuality only in his right to refuse to obey the ruler if it will mean the loss of his life. This

theoretical conception of society gives moral force to
that conception of society which sees it as literally a
'body politic' in which men fulfil different functions
just as different parts of the body fulfil different
functions but all being subject to the rule of the head.
In this conception of society the problem of equality
does not arise. It does not arise because all men are
seen as essential to the body politic, some may have
functions which are less prestigious than others but
these functions are none the less essential functions
and ones in which they can take pride (for a full
discussion of this point see Dumont, 1972). We see
this position as paradoxical — a hierarchical society
which does not raise the question of equality;
however, to most of those living in such a society the
situation is not paradoxical at all because the point of
reference is the society not the individual; the
individual does not exist except as a member of
society, which is why banishment was an effective
sanction in such societies, for to be banished was to
cease to have a social existence. Hobbes gave this
conception of society moral force by insisting that
for men to be true men they had to live in society
and society could only exist so long as men gave
obedience to a sovereign; it was therefore in men's
own interest to give this obedience, for without it
there would be a 'war of all against all'.

Contract Community

The concept of 'contract community' also starts

from assumptions about the nature of man, but
assumptions directly contrary to those of Hobbes. If
Hobbes saw men as inherently self-seeking, restrained
only by fear of the power of the sovereign, Rousseau
(1968) saw man as inherently good, 'a noble savage'
perverted by society. The point of reference for
Hobbes is the society and the problem one of
restraining the individual. The point of reference for
Rousseau is the individual and the problem one of
restraining society. Society is to be restrained by the
device of 'the contract'. Men are presumed to agree
to co-operate so long as society acts in their best
interests. When it no longer acts in their interest they
can argue that their contract with society or its ruler
is no longer valid and hence they can disobey society
or its ruler. Society exists to serve the individual.
However, such a conception of society creates severe
problems of social order for if each individual is free
to abrogate his contract at any time the result is
social anarchy. Rousseau was not an anarchist and so
he sought a solution to this problem and found it in
the mystical concept of 'general will'. For society to
exist men must agree to obey the 'general will' which
was not simply public opinion or majority decisions
but something containing elements of both and yet
existing as neither.

The concept of 'general will' re-emerges as the
concept of 'collective consciousness' in Durkheim's
(1933) attempts to explain social order. Durkheim
argues that social order can be maintained in two
ways. In the first instance it can be maintained by all
men obeying an agreed and unquestioned system of

values. Durkheim argues that such blind obedience to
a set of values is a characteristic of societies in which
all men are functionally equal. By this he means that
if an individual unit were to disappear the functioning
of society would not be affected for each individual
(or group) has the same set of skills to contribute
toward society. Because in this conception of society
the individual exists solely as an interchangeable cog
in the machine of society Durkheim characterises such
societies as ones exhibiting 'mechanical solidarity'.
(Mechanical solidarity is not the same as 'hierarchical
community' although there are many points of
similarity.) In both society is asserted as more
important than the individual and both rest on
traditional unquestioned values. However in a society
characterised by mechanical solidarity each individual
unit of the society is similar to every other unit
whereas in a 'hierarchical community' each unit
performs a differentiated function in the 'body politic'.
(If each individual can exist independently of
every other individual then the problem becomes one
of explaining why society exists.) Durkheim suggests
it is because all give unquestioned obedience to an
agreed set of values and this binds the individuals
together. In societies where men are not
functionally equivalent another mode of solidarity
prevails which he calls 'organic solidarity'. Where a
division of labour takes place then men become
functionally dependent on each other and this binds
society together. In this respect Durkheim's concept
of organic solidarity is similar to the Hobbesian
concept of the body politic. Where it differs is that

Durkheim does not argue that this mutual dependence requires the organising principle of hierarchy to sustain it as a society. Rather he argues that it requires a 'collective consciousness'. The parallel between Rousseau's 'general will' and Durkheim's 'collective consciousness' is quite striking; both are mystical concepts which are never clearly explained but are seen as co-ordinating mechanisms in societies occupied by rational men.

It is Durkheim's conception of 'organic solidarity' and Rousseau's conception of a society based on contract that is completely new. In both conceptions the individual is celebrated and in both the problem becomes one of explaining how society can exist when its key element is the celebration of individuality. The interesting feature of both answers is that neither suggests a structure of power and co-ordination because both are committed to individuality, Rousseau as an 'ought' and Durkheim as an 'is'. Valuing the individual means an egalitarian stance, for each individual has to be seen as unique and equally important and this means that no one individual can be valued more than any other. Unable to suggest or describe a structure that is egalitarian they both turn to the realm of ideas and values and posit a sovereign 'general will' or 'collective consciousness' to which men give obedience and which ensures co-ordination in society, for if all men are agreed on their values and ends then there is no need to force men to obey other men — all 'right thinking men' will act in concert.

The interesting question then arises, as to how one

ensures that men are aware of the 'general will' or
'collective consciousness' and the answer given by
both Rousseau, in *Émile* (1969), and Durkheim, in
Moral Education (1961), is that one brings them up
in the right way, one educates them. The difference
between the two men then becomes apparent. For
Rousseau education is centred on the individual and
is a means of developing the innate potential of the
individual. For Durkheim education is also centred on
the individual but is seen as a means of ensuring
that the individual adopts the values of his society —
the concern is to develop 'rational morality' so that
the pupil may understand the 'collective consciousness'.

Communitas

The last concept of community differs radically from
the previous two concepts. The first conception of
community, the 'hierarchical community' is a
conception that stresses social structure and social
position, and is bound up with tradition and stability.
The second conception, the 'contract community',
stresses the individual and is bound up with social
order. The third and last concept of community as
'communitas' stresses individuality to such an extent
that social structure, social position and even social
order are lost so that all is change and flux. Turner,
in his book *The Ritual Process* (1974, p.166) first
coins the term and points up what is meant by it by
contrasting it with a model of society which bears

most resemblance to the hierarchical community
discussed above:

> All human societies implicitly or explicitly refer
> to two contrasting social models. One . . . is of
> society as a structure of jural, political, and
> economic positions, offices, statuses, and roles, in
> which the individual is only ambiguously grasped
> behind the social persona. The other is of society
> as a communitas of concrete idiosyncratic
> individuals, who, though differing in physical and
> mental endowment, are nevertheless regarded as
> equal in terms of shared humanity. The first model
> is of a differentiated, culturally structured,
> segmented, and often hierarchical system of
> institutionalized positions. The second presents
> society as an undifferentiated, homogenous whole,
> in which individuals confront one another
> integrally, and not as 'segmentalized' into statuses
> and roles.

Like the 'contract community' this concept also
implies egalitarianism but it differs from that concept
of community in that it values change and instability:
spontaneity and immediacy are valued and the
problem of social order is only a problem in so far as
social order impedes such spontaneity.

Conclusion

The three different concepts of community each give

differential importance to individuality, differential importance to social structure and values and differential importance to stability or change. At one extreme lies the 'hierarchical community' where individuals are differentiated and evaluated as part of a functional organism, where stability is all-important and a hierarchical social structure based on power maintains that stability. This conception of community does not raise the problem of equality. In the middle lies the 'contract community' where individuals are celebrated as individuals, but where stability and order remain important and a mystical concept in the realm of ideas, the 'general will' or the 'collective consciousness', binds the society together. This conception of community implies egalitarianism. Finally there is the 'communitas' which celebrates individuality and instability and gives no importance or attention to social structure or values. Like the 'contract community' the 'communitas' implies egalitarianism.

Chapter 2

The School as a 'Hierarchical Community'

The origins of the educational concept of community lie in the public schools of the nineteenth century. The conception of community that was developed was that of the 'hierarchical community'. Social order takes primacy over the individual, tradition and stability are valued and the structure of the community is hierarchical. Equality is not a problem in such a conception for the emphasis is upon the school not the individual in it and the individual's importance lies in his potential to serve the school while he is in it and when he is outside it he exists solely as a representative of the school. The ultimate sanction of such a community, as it was in the body politic, is expulsion and exile.

The reasons for the idea of the English school as a 'hierarchical community' developing are historically specific (Baron 1955). The public schools when they were revitalised as competitive non-profit making businesses had to persuade the middle class

population of England to send their sons to them.
They therefore had to offer something to attract the
parents. What they offered was the promise that if
you sent your son to them they would turn him out
as a young gentleman fit to act as a leader in society.
This promise attracted both those who were
themselves gentlemen and wished their sons to be
confirmed in that status and also those who, although
rich, were not accepted as gentlemen and wished
their sons to acquire the social behaviour appropriate
to their wealth. It is not suggested that the schools,
or rather the headteachers and governors, sat down
and thought out the problem in this way but rather
that the successful schools were those who found the
formula to attract clients. That formula was the
liberal curriculum. The liberal or humanist tradition
had developed as a coupling of Christianity and the
Classical World. The humanist perspective saw the
prescripts of both the pagan ancients and the
Christian moderns as guides to living. The purpose of
a liberal education was to expose pupils to those
writings so that they could apply them in their own
lives. This liberal tradition had however become not
only a means of education but also a mark of status.
Those with a liberal education were those able to
devote time and resources to a study of Scripts.
Initially such study had been confined to the Church
but after the Renaissance it became much more the
prerogative of the nobility. The claim of the public
schools to teach in the liberal tradition was therefore
a dual claim: it was a claim to use a certain
curriculum but it was also a claim to endow status. It

was thus a very powerful selling point because it
attracted parents who saw the liberal curriculum as a
mark of education: probably clerics in the main;
those who saw it as a means of achieving status: the
aspiring merchants and industrialists; and those who
saw it as a means of confirming their status: the upper
classes (Wilkinson 1970). The result of the success of
the liberal curriculum as a selling point was that the
public schools attracted a population that was,
within the middle class category, heterogeneous with
regard to social class. The population was also heterogeneous geographically, first because the railways made
travel relatively easy and second because the schools
aimed to attract parents in a social category, the
middle classes, rather than parents in a geographical
region. (This does not deny a regional basis in the
recruitment of many schools.)

The adoption of a liberal curriculum had profound
consequences on the activities that took place in the
schools, because such a curriculum was concerned not
only with the intellect but also with the development
of the physical and the spiritual in the pupils. In short
it was concerned with the development of 'the whole
man'. The success of the liberal curriculum in
attracting clients also had profound consequences
because the clients that were attracted were socially
diverse and came from a wide geographical area. It
was necessary therefore to develop a mode of
education that was able to cope with the problems of
a diverse intake and also able to mould that intake of
pupils so that they could regularly and consistently
'turn out the leisured, pious, gentlemanly amateur'

(Mitchell 1964). The solution that emerged was the creation of a 'hierarchical community'.

The three concerns of the liberal curriculum became ways of asserting the hierarchical community. The intellect was fed on the classics which were oriented to epochs that were distant in both space and time and required for their understanding the mastery of dead languages. Such a curriculum cut off the pupils from the local community. They could not use the local area for examples to illustrate their texts nor could they talk to locals about their studies, only their peers in the school. The classical curriculum in this way isolated the school from the local area and made the school the only important community. The spiritual aspect of the liberal curriculum was met by compulsory worship. Such worship asserted the reality of the school community, for only school members attended. The chapel was the symbolic representation of the school as a separate community and the daily act of worship the ritual affirmation of that community. Perhaps most important of all the contributions of the liberal curriculum was that of sport. The concern with physical development derived directly from the classical tradition, for Ancient Greek education was concerned with developing the body as well as the mind, and with the motto of 'mens sana in corpore sano' (a healthy mind in a healthy body) the public schools threw themselves into the same endeavour. To the Greek concept of individual physical endeavour they added a contribution all their own: the team game. The team game was a brilliant social

invention because it provided in microcosm the
'hierarchical community': the rules of the game (the
social order) take precedence over the individual,
there is a hierarchical structure with the captain
having control but always remaining just one of the
units in the team, the individual is valued not for his
individuality but for his contribution to the team and
reference and loyalty are to the team not to the
individuals in it. The only aspect missing is a respect
for stability and this is provided by the rules of the
game. Such a powerful metaphor of the 'hierarchical
community' exercised great symbolic power in public
school life and, because ex-public schoolboys became
leaders in society, also in national life with phrases
like 'play the game', 'it's not cricket', 'pull together
as a team', for it epitomised that life and its values.

The social structure of the public school, that
developed to cope with a diverse intake, was the
social structure of a 'hierarchical community'. The
strong element of boarding in all public schools
meant that the school became the only life of the
pupils in it. The individual pupil had existence only
as a social category in the body politic: a fag, a
newcomer, a prefect. He had no life, or at least the
school recognised no life, outside the school. In the
school all his activities were regulated and controlled
by a routine. He was not allowed outside the total
society of the school, except at certain times, and
then with permission and an exhortation to
remember he was a representative of the school, so
that even when outside the school he did not become
an individual but was a school representative (for a

discussion of totality see Goffman, 1961). The school
provided social categories that the pupil filled so that
he had an identity within the 'hierarchical
community'. This use of school-based categories
meant that distinctions between pupils that they
brought with them from the outside world had to be
denied. This denial of differences upon entry into the
'hierarchical community' was also an excellent device
for moulding a heterogeneous intake into a
homogeneous output. The public schools therefore
insisted upon school uniform so that all would be
dressed alike and controlled the pupils' pocket money
so that all were equal in terms of wealth. The public
school accent fulfilled the same role by removing
dialect and therefore regional distinctions. This
assertion of uniformity and equality at first sight
appears to conflict with the fact that a 'hierarchical
community' has no problem of equality. It is however
only an apparent conflict for a hierarchical
community still has a problem of equity. It resolves
this problem by treating all those belonging to the
same social category as equals but it does not raise
the problem of equality between categories or
individuals. Uniforms are important not only for their
equalising function but also because they symbolic-
ally remove individual identity and make the pupil a
unit in the community and assert that communal
identity when he is outside the school. There were
not, however, only two categories of community
members, pupils and staff. Numerous other categories
were provided. For the pupils the two most
important were those of the school house and those

connected with authority positions. Both of these important categories can be traced back to aspects of the liberal tradition. The house system was an administrative device for ensuring pastoral care of the pupils; care for their spiritual and emotional development. The public schools were largely run by Anglican or Methodist ministers and both of these persuasions place emphasis upon the pastoral aspects of the minister's role. It created for the pupils a category within the larger body politic to which they could give allegiance. Just as team games provided a microcosm of the total school community so too did the house. In this way the school was formed of competing social groups all owing allegiance to the total community. The house system was a means of monitoring and developing the spiritual side of the 'whole man'. The various authority systems, prefects, house captains, fags, etc., fulfilled two functions. First, they enabled social order to be maintained without constant staff effort. Second, they were seen as a means of encouraging 'leadership qualities'. The public school concept of leadership meant that these qualities were not those of drive and initiative. The public schools were not concerned with industry where drive and initiative were needed. Rather they were concerned to produce gentlemen. Their pupils when they left school were expected to fill the role of leaders in a small local community of which the archetype was the Justice of the Peace. They were concerned therefore to produce men of good character, gentlemen, able to 'set an example'.

Leadership was expected to develop by giving

pupils posts of responsibility where they could exercise their powers of leadership. This leadership role was often compounded with prowess in team games: the head of house or head prefect was also often head of cricket and rugby. Team games were seen as particularly appropriate for developing the 'character' of pupils and the role of team captain, as it was expected to be exercised in public schools, was precisely the type of leader that was desired. In short the leaders the schools developed were not individualists but leaders in the stable 'hierarchical community' of the school who were expected to become leaders in the stable 'hierarchic community' of a locality upon leaving school.

The public school today remains a 'hierarchical community' with the head as the sovereign. Lambert (1968) in his study of public schools found that when compared with state schools the social order took primacy over the individual in that the pupils preferred social qualities rather than individual qualities (see Table 1), the school was seen to promote a herd instinct (see Table 1) and the heads preferred leavers oriented towards the collective rather than the individual (see Table 2). Similarly traditional values were more highly regarded (see Table 1), the structure of the community was more hierarchical (see Table 3) and the individual was expected to be loyal and committed to the school (see Table 1).

Although the public school remains more of a 'hierarchical community' than the state school, state schools also strove to be hierarchical communities because the public schools became the ideal to which

Table 1   Pupils' opinions (percentage response)

Boy boarders 16-18	State and integrated schools	Public schools
Social qualities preferred	39·0	47·6
Individual qualities preferred	59·0 (n = 284)	49·9 (n = 954)
School promotes herd instinct	11·0 (n = 353)	41·0 (n = 1,191)
Scale of acceptance 0- 6	33·0	12·2
of traditional 7-12	57·1	57·1
values (0 = no 13-18	9·4	28·9
acceptance) 19-20	0·0 (n = 284)	1·0 (n = 954)
Strongly committed	10·7	30·9
Committed	24·8	31·8
Qualified or no commitment	64·5 (n = 284)	37·3 (n = 954)

Source: Adapted from Tables 14, 16, 17, 30 in Lambert (1968).

Table 2   The collective and individual attributes preferred in school leavers[1]

	Public school heads (n = 22)	Integrated school heads (n = 7)	State school heads (n = 15)
Collectively oriented attributes	5·0	3·4	2·1
Individually oriented attributes	1·4	3·4	4·4

Source: Adapted from Table 18 in Lambert (1968).

1 The figures represent the frequency distribution derived from a content analysis of heads' responses in depth interviews.

Table 3   Pupil hierarchies in the house system

Distribution of official status among boys 16-18 according
to a score ranging from 0 = no official status to 30+ = high
status (total of scores for each status position held)

Scores	State and integrated schools	Public schools
0-10	63·4	37·0
11-20	29·6	33·1
21-30+	15·0 (n = 284)	29·9 (n = 594)

Source: Adapted from Table 13 in Lambert (1968).

all English schools subscribed. They became the
model for all schools because when state education
was expanded the schools with the highest status, the
grammar schools created by the 1907 Act, received as
heads men who had been teachers, and often house-
masters, in the public schools and they appointed as
teachers men who if they had not taught in a public
school had themselves been taught in such a school
before going to Oxford or Cambridge. In turn the
training colleges for teachers were staffed by
ex-grammar school teachers. These men made the
training colleges 'hierarchical communities' (Shipman
1967) and both in this way and by precept they
passed on the ideal to their students to carry into the
new secondary modern schools and later still the
comprehensive schools.

So pervasive is the concept in English education
that it is unthinkable to conceive of a school that is
not committed to the development of its pupils'
personalities, does not have a headteacher and does
not espouse and value the concept of the school as a

'hierarchical community'. The ideal school is spoken
of, by headteachers at speech days, as a ship —
isolated, hierarchical, total in its control of all aspects
of life and one in which the officers are concerned for
the welfare of the men. Of course state schools are
not isolated and nor do they have the total control
over all aspects of life so characteristic of a boarding
school or a military unit. Their 'hierarchical
community' remains therefore a pale copy of the
public school: lacking control over all their pupils'
lives they extend their control as far as they can by
the use of homework and the insistence upon the
wearing of uniform outside the school; lacking a full
house system they set up copies which often exist
solely as a means of dividing up the school into teams
for the sports day; lacking the full hierarchical
paraphernalia of a public school they none the less
create prefects, and monitors with powers, often
much more limited than those given to pupils in
public schools, to discipline other pupils. One thing
they do not lack — the conception of the headteacher
as the unchallengeable sovereign. Underlying all these
devices is the model of the public school and the
valuation of the school as a 'hierarchical community'.
This can be seen in the statements a sample of headteachers made about uniform and assembly (the
sample was representative of all secondary schools in
England and Wales; for a description of the sample
see King, 1973 and for a full list of statements see
Easthope, 1973) in which they were asked the purpose
of these devices: 64 per cent (n = 72) used terms such
as 'corporate', 'binds', 'members of one body', 'unity'

when discussing school assembly and 38 per cent
(n = 70) used similar forms when discussing school
uniform. The importance of uniform as an
affirmation of community is shown also by their
repeated assertion that the wearing of uniform was
a means of removing social differences, thus making
all members of the school equal. In this respect the
fact that most schools in the sample forbade the
wearing of badges of non-school organisations (King
1973) is a very significant demonstration of the way
the primacy of the school community is maintained.

One feature of the educational concept of
community that does not derive directly from the
concept of a 'hierarchical community' needs special
attention. This is the idea that the school to exist as
a community must be small. This is not a feature of
Hobbes's theoretical formulation of the concept
because he was concerned with the large state and, in
practice, states such as Mussolini's Italy in
particular, but also Hitler's Germany and Franco's
Spain, have existed as 'hierarchical communities'. The
idea that the 'hierarchical community' must be small
seems to be confined to the conceptualisation of the
school as a 'hierarchical community'. The reason for
this valuation of small size is related to the liberal
tradition. The concern of teachers is not only with
the intellects of their pupils but also their characters:
they are concerned with socialising the children who
enter the school. Socialisation, the development in
individuals of patterns of behaviour and a belief in
the correctness and goodness of those patterns, is
more apparent in infant schools (King 1969a) but it

none the less, because of the liberal tradition, remains a large element in secondary education. Socialisation has almost always been the prerogative of small groups. The family forms the fundamental small group for this purpose. Once the child moves outside the family it is the community of the tribe or village which develops a greater number and a wider variety of relationships but, even in the tribe and the village the scale is small — relationships are personal. In our society the school has taken the place of the village.

The development of large comprehensive schools presented teachers with a serious challenge to the idea of the school as a small community. Comprehensive schools, although not the only large schools, were the first schools that were expected to be large and were created to be large. The arguments for the introduction of the comprehensive school were ideological, economic and educational. The ideological arguments have no relevance to the debate over size although they are relevant to debates about hierarchy and they will be discussed in Chapter 4. Here however it is the economic and educational arguments that are at issue. The economic arguments for large schools are of two kinds. The first argument concerns the utilisation of resources and what might be called the 'economies of mass production' applied to education. This argument suggests that in large schools the amount of money needed for each pupil will be less because of savings achieved by avoiding duplication both of capital equipment and buildings. At the same time because the buildings and capital equipment are in one place they can be supplied to fulfil specialist needs. The second economic argument is that it is possible to provide for specialist needs because of the large number of pupils, e.g. it might be uneconomic to build a swimming pool for use by fifty children whereas it is economic to build it for over one thousand children. Similar reasoning applies to the employment of specialist teachers. The flaw in the economic argument is that it ignores existing capital investment in buildings. The educational argument for a large school was that a non-selective school if it were to have a viable sixth form would have to have a very large intake of pupils. This argument rested on two assumptions. First, it assumed that there was only a limited pool of ability suitable for sixth form work, the size of which could be calculated by looking at sixth forms in grammar schools. Donaghy (1971) is the latest in a long line of authors to challenge this assumption on the grounds that the greater expectations of pupils who are no longer branded as failures will lead to more pupils going into sixth forms in comprehensive schools than would have gone with a grammar/secondary modern system. Second, it assumed that sixth forms would remain purely as institutions for academic pupils interested in going to university or college. This has not proved to be the case. Sixth forms now deal with a wide ability range and a wide range of 'non-academic' subjects (Schools Council 1970).

Although the economic and educational arguments for large schools no longer seem convincing they were sufficiently convincing to lead many education authorities to build them as large institutions. Their size was perceived as a challenge to the perception of the school as a community. It was feared by the staff of these schools that it would become impossible to maintain close personal relationships with all pupils. Nor for that matter would it be possible for the head to know all the staff although this fact attracted less attention. Educationalists forecast that the large comprehensive schools would be impersonal cities rather than villages adding to the general impersonalised, routinised life of the adolescent in the modern world and pushing him towards delinquency (Wilson 1966). Faced with this situation, which was conceived of as a problem by heads, they utilised once again the structural forms developed in the public schools and created smaller units to act as small communities within the large community. These units were not always houses but were sometimes based on age divisions in the school such as upper and lower school. Whatever their basis they reinstate the concept of the school as a 'hierarchical community' with the pastoral care bases acting, as did the houses in the public schools, as organs of the body politic. The reinstatement of the concept of 'hierarchical community' was not the only response open to heads. In America the same problem was encountered as early as 1929 with the growth of large high schools. The American response was to create a separate pastoral role to deal solely with non-academic matters (Lynds 1929). Without a cultural notion of the school as a hierarchical community this separation has proceeded rapidly so that today there is a distinct profession of school guidance counselling.

It is interesting to see here a similar bifurcation of the
teaching role into pastoral and academic staff (Mays
1968) and the growth of school counselling courses in
universities. However the demand in England has not
been so great. The reason for this is not, as Rowe
(1969) suggests, that headteachers are afraid of a
curtailing of their power but because the need is
already presumed to have been met by the structural
forms of the 'hierarchic community' in the form of
house and age based pastoral care systems. Whether
their forms have met the need to avoid impersonality
or whether there was no need there at all is difficult
to ascertain, but empirical evidence, limited though it
is, suggests that pupils do not feel less cared for in
large schools (Ross 1972) and are as favourably
disposed toward their schools as those in smaller
schools (Ross 1972, King 1973). The staff in schools
appear to respond differentially to an increase in size:
women staff noticing a decline in communal feelings
in larger schools — recording staff relationships as less
caring, less helpful, less friendly and generally bad —
more than staff in smaller schools, whereas men only
noted an increase in formality and they did not
evaluate this as necessarily bad (Easthope 1973).

Conclusion

Whatever the reactions of pupils or teachers, the
structural forms that have been developed to meet
what was perceived as a problem of size have
remained those that contribute to a 'hierarchical

community'. The model is still the body politic with the head as sovereign holding sway over a community composed of differentiated social categories. Social order takes primacy over the individual and the individual is recognised not as an idiosyncratic organism but as a person occupying social categories whose first loyalty is to the body politic. In this conception the question of equality is a question of fair treatment to all in the same social category requiring uniform behaviour from the sovereign, so that all in a category are equally treated.

Chapter 3

The Sovereign Head

Inextricably bound up with the concept of the school as a 'hierarchical community' is the idea of the head as its sovereign. International comparisons (see for example Sharma 1963) demonstrate clearly that the position of the head in the English school is unusual in the power and responsibility it gives to one individual in a school:

A school is what its headmaster makes of it; no matter how much decentralisation, how much diffusion of authority and influence there may be, it is the influence of the headmaster that is for better or worse, the principal formative agent (a public school headmaster cited by Weinberg, 1969).

Just as the idea that the school is a 'hierarchical community' has historically specific roots so too has the conception of the head as its sovereign (Baron

1970). During the early years of the nineteenth
century schools began to grow in size. Schools that
had once consisted of a master and his pupils became
conglomerates of many masters and many pupils.
Some form of administrative co-ordination was seen
as necessary. Several forms were tried, e.g. Liverpool
Collegiate had a committee of masters who took it in
turns to deal with the organisation of the school.
However the form of co-ordination that was
eventually adopted in all schools was that of a head
appointed for life. This form of co-ordination won
out over the other forms for two reasons. First, it was
in accord with the methods of industrial organisation
prevalent at that time. Britain led the world in
industrial production and it seemed appropriate to
apply the methods that had proved successful in
industry to the school. These methods had involved
an entrepreneur able to act with few societal
constraints in pursuit of profit. In the school this
meant a head with extensive freedom of action. Like
Victorian employers heads were given the powers to
choose their materials, their methods and their
employees and to organise these in any fashion they
deemed appropriate to achieve profit. This meant
that the head chose the curriculum, the methods of
teaching it and the staff to carry out that teaching.
His power over his staff was immense and involved
appointment, promotion and dismissal. Not until an
act of 1908 were the assistant masters other than paid
servants of the head, responsible directly to him and
subject to instant dismissal. Today the head still
controls appointments in fact, although nominally

it is a responsibility of the governors, and promotion within the school remains within the head's direct power while promotion outside it is indirectly controlled by the use of references. The conception of the head as an educational entrepreneur meant that the role of the head was seen to be that of an organiser rather than a scholar. His ability as an entrepreneur was judged by his success in attracting pupils and/or obtaining scholarships for his pupils. This was often tied to his salary so that the more pupils a head attracted to his school the higher his salary became, thus building in the profit motive directly (in the public sector the profit motive was built in with 'payment by results'). The second reason for co-ordination by a single autocratic ruler stemmed from the success of Arnold of Rugby. Arnold's creation of the school as a 'hierarchical community' and the success of that creation led to it becoming the model for many other schools. The concept of 'hierarchical community', as developed in Rugby, implied a sovereign (Hobbes's conception implied absolute sovereignty but this was not necessarily vested in one man) and the adoption of the Rugby model therefore implied an adoption of the head as sovereign.

The freedom of the head to act as he saw fit did not however only lead to a scramble by heads to make the maximum profits. Great individual heads, such as Arnold and Thring, used their power (given to them by society as a means of controlling them by forcing them to continually seek profit and avoid laziness) to resist societal pressures. The head's power became a counterweight to the power of society and enabled, and enables, heads to pursue educational ends against societal pressures. The innovators in English education could not have put many of their ideas into practice without the freedom from social pressure that the role of head gives. This conception of the role of the head as a champion of educational values became institutionalised with the creation of a pressure group to resist state interference in the public schools, the Headmasters' Conference.

Interestingly, just as size led to problems of co-ordination which were resolved by the creation of the role of head, so today the large comprehensive schools have produced a reassessment of the head's role because of the difficult problems of co-ordination in large organisations. Many head-teachers of large comprehensive schools have argued that they have to delegate some of their powers (see, for example, Conway 1970, Percival 1968, Miles 1968). Sociologists and educationalists have argued that the role of the head will change. Three aspects of the role can be distinguished: (a) the instrumental, a concern with task performance and thus administrative co-ordination, (b) the expressive, a concern with reducing tensions amongst pupils and teachers and the generation of a spirit of harmony and (c) the symbolic, the head as a symbol of the school and its authority both within the school and with respect to the outside world. The IAAM (1960) have suggested that the head will have to delegate the instrumental aspects retaining the expressive and the symbolic; King (1968) has suggested he may retain the

instrumental aspects delegating the symbolic;
Burnham (1968) agrees with King that the head
will retain the instrumental aspects but stresses the
delegation of the expressive aspects and Taylor
(1968) puts forward the contrary view that the head
will retain the expressive aspects and delegate the
instrumental. It is apparent that there is little
agreement on the changes that can be expected
only agreement that there will be changes in the
large comprehensive schools.

It is understandable that there is little agreement,
for a change in the role of the head implies a change
in the power available to him and/or the way he
exercises that power and power is a deceptively
simple but in fact an extremely complex concept.
The powerful have been variously defined as those
who express the values of the group (Parsons cited in
Giddings 1968), those who occupy key positions in a
communications network (Barnard 1938, Burns 1954,
Tronc 1967, Bales 1950), those who take decisions
(D'Antonio and Erickson 1962, Dahl 1961, Homans
1951, Miller 1958), those with a say in decision
making (Tannenbaum 1956, 1961, 1962), those who
can draw on resources (Stinchcombe 1968, Etzioni
1961, Mechanic 1962, Goss 1961, Glaser 1963, Moore
1921, Lippit 1952), those who control others (Weber
1964, Goldhamer and Shils 1939, Katz and Kahn
1966) and those with freedom of action (Abramson
1958, Bierstedt 1950). Faced with the complexities
of these numerous definitions the difficulty of
looking empirically at the changing power of the head
is apparent. However an empirical study was

undertaken with power defined as control over a situation, a conception of power that subsumes the last five conceptions in the list above (Easthope 1973). Control over a situation meant that an individual could redefine a situation *and* have this redefinition accepted by others (if it is not accepted then the individual would be labelled as 'mad' and would be controlled by others). A person was seen as having power therefore if he decided on any aspect of a situation — its abolition or introduction; the distribution of objects, people, time and space in that situation. He had authority if his approval was necessary before a decision taken by another person was implemented; he had influence if he was consulted before a decision was taken and he had autonomy if he could take a decision without seeking approval. Using these definitions a study of a grammar school, a secondary modern school and a large comprehensive school was undertaken. The results in each school were similar: the head was the man with the most control (Table 11 gives a full table of results). The exercise of that control differed in each school however: the secondary modern school head took decisions and exercised direct power, the grammar school head relied instead on authority and the comprehensive school head sat on committees of senior staff and thus shared his power without delegating it. It is interesting to speculate how far the different modes of exercising control were the products of different types of school and how far the products of the individual personalities of the heads concerned. Cohen's work (1970) on headteachers

which found that heads in larger schools are more
likely to use authority suggests the differences may
have been a product of personality rather than school
type. Regardless of the differences the interesting
feature of the results was the maintenance of the
conception of the head as sovereign even in the large
comprehensive school. An observation of a staff
meeting in the large comprehensive demonstrated
this clearly. The meeting took place in one of the
school halls on a hot evening in June immediately
after school. The head, the deputy head and the
senior mistress sat behind a long table in front of the
stage on the floor of the hall facing the staff who sat
or stood in a semi-circle. After some preliminary
routine administrative matters were dealt with the
meeting suddenly came to life over an announcement
about the school fête. The fête had been a regular
feature of the school year and the decision to hold it
again was taken at a meeting of parents and elected
staff representatives. Some staff objected to being
committed to the fête without being asked. After
more objections were made about the disruption the
fête caused, the head took the decision not to hold
the fête. The interesting point about this decision is
that none of the staff disputed the head's right to
take it, although they had just objected to not being
consulted by their elected representatives. However
one member of staff pointed out that the decision of
the head meant that the elected staff representatives
were not being supported. At this point a vote was
suggested. The head objected to a vote but agreed to
a 'show of hands'. Once again no one disputed his

right to decide whether or not to take a vote. The
'show of hands' was very close with 31 for the fête,
29 against. The head asked for time and said he
would give them his decision the next day. Again his
right to take this decision was not disputed. The
observation of the meeting, because of the conflict it
demonstrates between the autocratic right of the
head to take decisions and the democratic ideology
that decisions should be taken by elected
representatives or a majority vote, illustrates in a very
clear way that the concept of the head as the
sovereign of a 'hierarchical community' remains an
integral part of the English education system even in
a large comprehensive school where a challenge to it
might be expected.

Conclusion

The power exercised by the head in an English school
is formidable, and the head can be compared to the
sovereign of a state whose powers are limited only by
the willingness of his subjects to obey his commands
but whose right to give commands is not disputed by
his subjects. Such a powerful figure was an historical
creation of the nineteenth century. The growth in
size of educational establishments in the nineteenth
century necessitated some form of co-ordination. The
autocratic head was the form adopted because it was
congruent with the most successful organisations in
nineteenth-century England, the industrial factories
which were run by autocratic entrepreneurs and

within education the example of the 'hierarchical community' of Rugby presupposed a sovereign ruler. Problems of size also face large comprehensive schools today and it has been suggested that such schools would lead to a diminution of the power of the head. This has not occurred because the school is still conceived of as a 'hierarchical community' and such a conception requires a sovereign head. One of the paradoxes of the great power that is given to heads is that although it was originally given to encourage them to fulfil societal goals it gives them sufficient resources to resist societal pressures and even to act against societal goals.

Part 2

Hierarchy

Chapter 4

Four Ideologies against Hierarchy

In this chapter the ideological arguments against hierarchical orders will be examined. The term ideology is not used in a pejorative sense. It means here an intellectual position held by a group of people from which they criticise others' actions and legitimate their own activities.

Two attacks upon hierarchic ordering in schools can be distinguished. The first, which can be denoted by the term 'social equality', argues that people in the same social category should be treated equally. It differs from the position discussed in Chapter 2 only in that its point of reference is not the school but the total society. Those arguing for social equality argue that there should be equal treatment for all teachers and all pupils in our society. The argument for equal treatment for all teachers is usually based on the ideology of professionalism. The argument for equal treatment for all pupils is one variant of the comprehensive ideology. The second attack, which

can be given the name 'social egalitarianism', argues
that people should be treated as individuals and the
purpose of education is the development of the
individual's potential. Those arguing for social
egalitarianism base their positions either on a Marxist
conception of the individual or on a conception of
the individual derived from Rousseau and the other
Romantic philosophers. The positions based on
Marxist writings give rise to the deschooling
ideologies whereas those based on the Romantic
tradition give rise to the progressive education
ideologies, which form the basis of the other variant
of the comprehensive ideology. The argument for
the development of the individual can be seen as
ranged along a continuum at one end of which lies
social anarchism and the concept of 'communitas'
where there is no structure, no hierarchy and no
evaluation, and at the other end lies the 'contract
community' with less structure, hierarchy and
evaluation than in a 'hierarchical community' but still
some.

The ideology of professionalism has two faces.
With regard to clients the ideology is hierarchical: the
professional is seen to have expert knowledge and
skills which are not available to the client. This
enables the professional to redefine the client's
problems in technical language and thus to label
the client, e.g. the doctor interprets the pains of a
man as a particular illness syndrome and labels the
man as a 'diabetic' or a teacher interprets the
performance of a child in an academic test and labels
him 'stupid'. This labelling has profound

consequences for clients affecting their behaviour from that point onwards. This hierarchical aspect of the ideology of professionalism is attacked by all the social egalitarian ideologies and will be discussed later. The other face of the ideology of professionalism is non-hierarchical. The possession of expert knowledge and skills places the professional above his clients but it places him on a par with his fellow professionals: the professional ideology insists that all certificated professionals are equally competent. What this implies is that all those who are identified as being in the social category 'professional teachers' should be treated equally. Where this social category includes all teachers in a society this has important implications. It means that all teachers regardless of what they teach, whom they teach or where they teach should be treated as equals and that criteria other than the identity of a teacher as a professional are irrelevant. In practice this ideology should mean a commitment to the same salary scale for all teachers regardless of the subject they teach, the age and ability of the pupils taught, the type of school they teach in, the colour or religion of the teacher. It is in fact an assertion that the only important identity of the professional teacher is that of a teacher not that of a history teacher or a wood-work teacher, a primary school teacher or a secondary school teacher, a grammar school teacher or a secondary modern school teacher, a teacher in Durham or a teacher in Norwich, a man or a woman, a black or a white, a Catholic or a Muslim. The multitudinous differentiations amongst teachers which

form the basis for hierarchic orderings are denied. In
fact the salaries of teachers differ widely in spite of
the expressed ideology. They differ for four reasons.
First, they differ because there is no agreement on
who should be included in the social category
professional teacher: there are different salary scales
for school teachers, teachers in further education and
teachers in higher education. Even within the
category school teacher there is dispute with one
union, the National Association of Schoolmasters,
arguing that different salaries should be paid to those
who are career teachers (i.e. have a record of
continuous teaching), and hence, it is implied, are the
only professional teachers. Second, they differ
because teachers are state employees in organisations
and as such have a position in a beaucracy and thus
have a bureaucratic career with higher salaries going
to more experienced functionaries and to those who
occupy administrative positions. Third, they differ
because there are other ideologies than the
professional ideology which are subscribed to by
many teachers, e.g. many teachers see themselves as
scholars and the task of education as encouraging
scholarship (Kob 1961) and therefore consider those
teaching the more academic subjects should have
higher salaries and better chances of promotion.
Finally there are differences stemming from market
forces, e.g. science graduates until recently usually
got high salaries very early in their teaching career,
London teachers and those teaching the handicapped
are paid more to attract teachers to these areas of
shortage. In spite of the reality of hierarchy, a reality

that will be discussed again in the next chapter, the ideology of professionalism remains as a source of legitimation for groups within education wishing to create equality between teachers.

Those seeking equality between pupils seek their legitimation in one variant of the comprehensive ideology. Like the professional ideology which asserts that the only important identity of the teacher is that of teacher, the comprehensive ideology based on arguments of equality (which will be referred to as the equitable comprehensive ideology from now on to distinguish it from the egalitarian comprehensive ideology described later) insists that the only important identity of the pupil is that of pupil. Identities such as sex, colour, religion or, importantly, social class are seen as irrelevant. The only relevant criteria for judgment are related to the pupil identity, i.e. academic ability.

Those supporting this ideology have been particularly concerned with the social class biases in the education system which mean that children of higher social classes have more chance of succeeding in education than children of lower classes even when measured ability is similar. (This relationship between social class and educational opportunity has been the main concern of the sociology of education since 1945; for a good discussion of the relationship see Swift 1973). To overcome these biases supporters of the ideology pressured for grants to enable working class children to continue in education — the scholarship system — and later instituted moves that led to free secondary education for all. However evidence in the 1950s and 1960s, both in government reports (Crowther 1960) and in sociological journals (Floud and Halsey 1957) demonstrated that the system of free secondary education that had been instituted, with selection by a battery of intelligence tests for grammar and secondary modern schools, continued to have a social class bias. The supporters of the ideology therefore began to campaign for the abolition of the selection tests and the abolition of the different schools the pupils were selected for, and their replacement by a universal system of comprehensive secondary schools. The overriding concern of the proponents of the equitable comprehensive ideology with social class has meant that the renunciation of other identities held by children coming into secondary schools has passed almost unnoticed, e.g. comprehensive schools are overwhelmingly mixed schools and this has been achieved with few disputes.

The practical implication of the equitable comprehensive ideology is that all pupils should go to similar schools. The means of achieving this have given rise to almost as much debate as the ideology itself. Similar schools mean similar staff, similar curriculums, similar pupils — for the composition of a school's intake is a vital characteristic of any school — and similar finance. Similar staff and similar curriculums present severe problems, particularly if the school is seen as an autonomous 'hierarchical community' in which the head is sovereign. With this conception of the school each head is free to select his own staff and his own curriculum. Even more

difficult however is the need to provide each school
with a similar set of pupils. Pupils differ in any one
local authority area in terms of sex, social class,
ability and sometimes colour. At the same time there
are geographical concentrations of pupils according to
social class and colour. To ensure that all schools
receive similar intakes some local education
authorities both in Britain and the USA either adjust
what are called the schools' 'catchment areas' so that
a 'balanced intake' is achieved in each school or
practise some form of 'busing' whereby pupils are
taken from the area in which they live to go to school
in another area, even though there may be a school in
their own area (see Coleman 1973, Armor 1973).

Finance, in Britain, is tied to pupil numbers and
particularly to the age composition of the pupil body,
older pupils giving the head more finance; a school
that retains its older pupils is therefore at an
advantage financially. To ensure equality of finance it
is therefore necessary to create a balanced intake by
one of the means discussed above, catchment areas or
busing, or to separate out the older pupils from the
younger. If the latter procedure is followed and 'short
course comprehensives' for 12-16-year-olds are
created each school receives similar finance and all
pupils in that age group are given equal financial
provision (King 1974).

The relationship of a school to its local area is a
problem that is raised, but in an entirely different
sense, by the deschooling ideology. The more extreme
variant of this ideology, as propounded by Ivan Illich
(1971), will be examined before looking at the less

extreme variants put forward by Douglas Holly
(1972) and Kenneth Richmond (1973). The ideology
rests upon a Marxist notion of individuality.
According to Marx (cited in Bottomore and Rubel
1963, p.90) the individual only realises his humanity
through labour:

> it is men, who, in developing their material
> production and their material intercourse, change,
> along with this their real existence, their thinking
> and the products of their thinking. Life is not
> determined by consciousness but consciousness by
> life.

However this humanity is denied by the fact that
men in a capitalist society are 'alienated' from their
labour: they have no control over the pace they work
at, the tools they use, the quality of the product they
produce or the choice of the product itself. Their
work is thus outside their control and is seen therefore as something entirely separate from their real
selves (ibid., p.69):

> Labour is external to the worker i.e. it does not
> belong to his essential being . . . the worker
> therefore only feels himself outside his work and
> in his work he feels outside himself . . . [work] is
> therefore not the satisfaction of a need, it is merely
> a means to satisfy needs external to it.

Illich applies this Marxian concept of alienation to
mental labour. He argues that a system of education

which enforces attendance at schools alienates both pupils and teachers from the products of their mental labour. Compulsory school attendance, Illich claims, signals to the pupil and to the rest of society that school knowledge is superior to other forms of knowledge, otherwise there would be no point in enforcing attendance. (Legally attendance at school is not compulsory, it is education approved by the state that is compulsory but in practice, for the majority of children, compulsory education means compulsory school attendance.) In this way the school marks off certain aspects of reality and gives them value over other aspects of reality. This constitutes what Illich calls the 'hidden curriculum' of schools: the existence of an organisation to which all children must go before becoming adults and in which they are taught knowledge, implies that what goes on within the school and its grounds is more important than what goes on outside those walls and grounds; it says 'learning *about* the world is more important than learning *from* the world' (Illich in Buckman 1973, p.10). This 'hidden curriculum' means that knowledge becomes a commodity and the task of teaching that of packaging the commodity so that it will appeal to the consumers, the pupils. As a commodity it is inevitably scarce, which implies limited access and a consequential hierarchy of knowledge consumers. This 'new class structure' based on possession of certificates of knowledge consumption Illich finds as depressing as a class structure based upon economic factors. To avoid the alienation of knowledge from the individual, Illich

argues, it is necessary to give back to the individual
control over knowledge production. This implies
what he calls 'deschooling society' by which he means
'above all the denial of professional status for the
second-oldest profession, namely teaching' (Illich
p.13, Buckman 1973). The deschooling ideology
seeks to give back to the individual control over the
production of knowledge and in so doing attacks the
hierarchy between professional teacher and pupil
client, by calling for the abolition of schools and the
abolition of teachers as professionals.

This conception of the school as an alien
institution into which local children enter has been
interestingly challenged recently by the development
of 'community schools'. Some new schools, usually
comprehensive schools, have sought to bring the local
community within the school, so that the school is
no longer an alien institution to the area in which it
is sited. The school is to be not only a 'hierarchical
community' in itself but also the core of the local
community. (This conception of the school is
associated with the concept of 'open education'
which seeks to break down boundaries both within
the school and between the school and the outside
world — see Chapters 6 and 7.) Part of the desire to
create 'community schools' stems from enlightened
self-interest: pupils will be more amenable to
discipline and perform better with parental interest.
In a sense the school tries to bring the local area
inside the 'nod-line', that point where people are on
nodding acquaintance (Goffman 1963), at which
point crime is lower because everyone knows each

other. Part of the desire stems also from a romantic ideal of community which relates back to the Cambridge colleges of the 1930s and the romanticism of William Morris (see Poster 1971, who argues for community schools). Interestingly such schools are usually sited in new housing estates occupied by the working class. The assumption made is that the school has cultural gifts to bring to the deprived locality. The school becomes a coloniser of the local area using the area as a source of ideas for an audience comprised of an élite drawn from inside and outside the area (the classic example of this process is Dartington Hall in Devon). Such a conception of a community school, as Illich would be the first to point out, far from destroying the hierarchy between school and local area only serves to strengthen it. A community school that is not a coloniser is difficult to conceive of in Britain because the concept of the school as an autonomous 'hierarchical community' with a sovereign head precludes any real local control over the process of education. However the autonomy of the school in England is seen as a benefit by those supporting the less extreme form of the deschooling ideology. These moderate deschoolers agree with Illich that school knowledge is alienated but argue that this alienation is not a product of compulsory schooling but a product of our society. Our society demands that the schools act as a sieve for talent and the rewards of our society go to those who gain certificates of knowledge. This, argues Holly (1972), leads to an instrumental attitude to schooling on the part of the pupils who see school either as a place to collect certificates or as an irrelevancy; both are the products of alienation. The autonomy of the school in England means however that schools can to some extent separate themselves from the demands of society. This relative autonomy means the possibility of free labour rather than alienated labour. For the moderate deschoolers therefore the answer does not lie in the abolition of schools but in a strengthening of them in their autonomous actions so that they can resist the pressures of a society committed to alienated knowledge, and teach in such a way as to bring knowledge back under the control of the learner.

It is the teaching process itself that is the concern of the progressive ideology. The individual child in the progressive ideology is conceived of as innately good and the task of education is to provide the environment in which that goodness can develop. Just as Rousseau's noble savage was seen to be better than modern civilised man corrupted by civilisation so the innocent child is seen to be better than the child corrupted by education. The parallels with Rousseau are however deeper than the replacement of the noble savage with the innocent child. Starting with the works of Rousseau, there was in the nineteenth century a movement in philosophy and art that has been labelled the 'Romantic Movement'. This Romantic Movement 'discovered' nature and valued the natural over the artificial, freedom over constraint and individual expression over societal conformity. In literature its classic exponents were the Romantic poets of the nineteenth century — Wordsworth,

Keats, Shelley, Byron, Tennyson. In education the
Romantic Movement had little influence until after
the First World War. Two developments led to its
adoption in education. The first was the war itself.
The war had sickened many intellectuals and they
were led to reject the societal values that had
produced the war. They cast around for a new
morality based on love and respect and found it in the
the Romantic Movement (Selleck 1972). The second
was the impact of Freudian and neo-Freudian
psychology. Freudian psychology gave 'scientific'
legitimation to the claim that men were constrained
by their society; they were 'repressed'. It therefore
became the task of education to free men from their
self-imposed 'repressions'. The practical exposition of
the progressive ideology was typified by (a) a stress
upon freedom and individuality which implied mild
discipline and a lack of competition, (b) communal
living with modified self-government (a 'contract
community'), (c) a stress upon craft in the curriculum
to encourage 'self-expression' (an important word in
the rhetoric of progressive education) and (d) the
siting of the schools of the movement in beautiful
countryside or at the very least having gardens in the
school (Selleck 1972).

The placing of the progressive ideology as a
development, in practice, of the Romantic Movement
is not meant to imply that the progressive schools
developed from a coherent philosophical position.
What is implied is that there was a congruence of
ideas between the Romantic Movement in philosophy
and art and the ideas that were used to justify the

practice of progressive education. The ideas of
individuality, freedom and growth which were the
key ideas of both the Romantic Movement and the
progressive ideology were developed in the
progressive schools from practice rather than any
developed philosophy. The radical schools and school
teachers set up their schools and their methods of
teaching and then were forced to defend their
methods from the attacks of teachers using traditional
methods. Their ideology, therefore, was developed in
a negative rather than a positive manner in response
to criticism of their methods and often took, and
takes, the form of pointing out the faults of
traditional methods rather than creating a coherent
ideology to support progressive methods. The
romantic ideology is, therefore, inferred from their
criticism of traditional methods and their practice of
progressive methods. It thus seems sensible to
describe progressive education in the way its
practitioners have described it, by contrasting its
methods and assumptions with a caricature of
traditional teaching methods. In this way the
assumptions of each method can be drawn out for
each has different philosophies and psychologies and
consequently different conceptions of learning,
different conceptions of knowledge and different
conceptions of the teacher-pupil relationship.

Traditional education is 'idealist' in the
philosophical sense of that word: it is based on the
assumption of an objective world 'out there' in which
facts exist independently of man. Progressive
education is 'phenomenological': it is based on the

assumption that men construct reality. These philosophies imply two different psychologies. The idealist
conception leads the psychologist to look at how men
perceive the world, how they select some perceptions
rather than others and how men can be trained to
learn some facts rather than others. The emphasis is
upon man as a receiver of information. The concern
of traditional education is with teaching pupils how
to discriminate amongst the information they are
receiving. The two fields most closely associated with
traditional teaching are, therefore, psychometrics,
which measures how well men have learnt the facts,
and behaviourism, which seeks to manipulate men so
that they can learn better. The phenomenological
conception leads the psychologist to look at how men
create their world. The emphasis is upon learning as a
process in which men interact and experiment with
their environment and each other. The fields
connected with phenomenology are, therefore,
developmental psychology, particularly that of Piaget,
and clinical observational psychology, which tries to
observe how men behave 'naturally' rather than
manipulating them experimentally.

In educational terms this means that learning is
conceived of entirely differently by traditional and
progressive teachers. They emphasise two different
aspects of the learning process: the receipt of
information is given primacy in traditional teaching,
the use of information to construct new ideas is given
primacy in progressive education. To caricature the
positions of both sides in the argument, for the
traditional teacher learning is an act in which the

individual takes in the knowledge object placed
before him whilst for the progressive teacher it is a
process during which the individual experiments with
the world. There are obviously, therefore, two
differing conceptions of education: the traditional
teacher is concerned with the knowledge objects, the
curriculum, whilst the progressive teacher is
concerned with the child. (It is for this reason that
the two patterns of education are sometimes
described as curriculum centred and child centred.)
There are thus two conceptions of knowledge: the
traditional teacher sees knowledge as arranged in
structures in which some knowledge is more valued
than others (a more recent version of this viewpoint
emphasises a hierarchy of mental skills rather than a
hierarchy of contents (Bloom 1956-65)) and he sees
his task, therefore, as one of best presenting that
knowledge so that it can be understood by the child;
the progressive teacher sees knowledge as actively
created by man and, therefore, sees his task as
providing the child with access to materials so that he
can create knowledge.

Just as the philosophy implies the psychology and
the psychology implies a conception of learning
which in turn implies a conception of knowledge, so
the differing conceptions of learning and knowledge
imply differing relationships between pupil and
teacher. The teacher's task in traditional education is
to mediate between the knowledge structure 'out
there' and the child in the classroom. He is an
interpreter of the corpus of knowledge, a master of
his subject who introduces others to its structure

and form. The teacher's task in progressive education on the other hand is to provide the child with the materials, experience and skills that will enable him to construct knowledge. He is a guide and provider in a land that is almost as foreign to him as it is to the child. He is judged successful when he learns from the child rather than the child learning from him.

In its extreme form therefore the progressive ideology is an attack upon all forms of hierarchy. The individual child and his or her development is the only important focus of attention: the task of education is the development of the idiosyncratic individual. By stressing the individuality of each child the ideology suggests there can be no hierarchies of merit, for if each child is unique it makes no sense to compare him with others on a scale of merit. By emphasising that learning is a process undertaken by the individual child it suggests that there can be no hierarchy of knowledge in which some subjects or skills should be more highly valued than others, for each individual will evaluate aspects of knowledge structures differently and it is the individual's evaluation which is central, for it is the individual child who is engaged in the process of learning. The emphasis upon the individual child as the only judge of his own learning and the emphasis upon freedom means that there cannot be any teacher-pupil relation-ship that is at all hierarchical: A.S.Neill (cited on p.48 of Selleck 1972) expressed this aspect of the ideology when he said 'Smash a window . . . chuck books about the room . . . anything to break this idea you are an exalted being.'

Logically therefore the progressive ideology implies 'communitas': the celebration of individuality to the exclusion of all forms of structure. In practice the ideology when applied has more closely resembled a 'contract community' in which there is structure but a structure that exists on sufferance of the members of the community. The logical application of the progressive ideology, its application in its extreme form, is ultimately anti-intellectual and anti-rational for if there are no criteria by which to judge thought and ideas, and there can be no such criteria if individuality is all, then there is no way of judging the ideology itself. An acceptance of the ideology can therefore only be made on mystical, non-rational grounds. The moderate expression of the progressive ideology also celebrates the individual and sees education as the process whereby the individual is given the maximum opportunity to develop free of artificial constraints imposed by society. Where it differs from the extreme viewpoint is in the insistence that, although the individual must be allowed to develop his potential freely, ultimately that development has to be judged in societal terms. The extreme variant stresses structureless equality. The moderate variant stresses equality of opportunity, that peculiar doctrine which asks that people be given the equal opportunity to be unequal: the individual must be given the opportunity to develop his full potential but once he has developed his potential he must be judged on societal criteria.

Those supporting the equality of opportunity variant of the progressive ideology may be characterized as supporters of the egalitarian comprehensive ideology. Unlike the proponents of the equitable comprehensive ideology, who argue that equal provision should be made for all pupils, the supporters of the egalitarian comprehensive ideology argue for unequal provision. They argue in fact for provision related to the individual child's needs, provision that will enable the child to develop his full potential (on this point they gain strange allies, those economists and politicians whose reference is not the individual but the society and who argue that society needs to develop the full potential of all its citizens to survive as a society). In practice the provision of unequal provision is usually made to groups, which are seen to be handicapped, rather than individuals. The system of positive discrimination whereby Negroes are guaranteed places at some colleges in the USA even where their performance is lower than white applicants is an example of the principle of inequality to produce equality, and in Britain the Educational Priority Areas projects whereby certain areas of cities, which are seen to be deprived, are given extra resources is another (see Midwinter 1972).

The difficulty with the concept of equality of opportunity is that of knowing when to apply societal criteria. If a child's development is prejudged then this may result in a stunting of his development: if a child is continually told he is stupid he may begin to believe it. (For evidence on self-fulfilling prophecies see Rosenthal and Jacobsen 1968.) At one time it was accepted that the decision should be taken at eleven years of age with the selection tests for grammar

school. This has now been strongly challenged and
the decision is delayed, often until fourteen years of
age when the child decides whether or not to take
external examinations and which external examinations to take. Julienne Ford (1969) has suggested that
there should be a distinct break between education
where no evaluation is made of the individual and
selection which is solely concerned with evaluation,
by the creation of two sets of institutions, 'schools'
for education up to fourteen years of age and colleges
for selection from fourteen years onwards. Robin
Pedley (1969) argues, however, that selection and
evaluation should be delayed until after higher
education and that the comprehensive school should
lead to the comprehensive university. Like the
moderate form of the other egalitarian ideology, that
of deschooling, the moderate form of the progressive
ideology faces the conflict between individual
development and societal pressures and, like the
moderate deschooling ideology, sees the solution in
the autonomy of the school. In both conceptions the
school asserts its independence so that it can
concentrate on education rather than evaluation.

Conclusion

Six attacks upon hierarchies in education have been
distinguished in this chapter. The first two attacks
are applications of the idea of equality to all teachers
and all pupils. Both the professional ideology, which
underlies the attack upon hierarchies amongst teachers,
and the equitable comprehensive ideology, which
underlies the attacks upon hierarchies between pupils,

call for a lack of hierarchy between schools: all
schools are expected to be similar. The remaining four
attacks which are applications of the idea of egalitarianism and thus the celebration of individuality can be
distinguished by their conceptions of individuality.
The deschoolers, both extreme and moderate, start
from a Marxist conception of the individual and see
the individual as alienated from his intellectual labour.
The extreme deschoolers locate the cause of this
alienation in compulsory schooling, the moderate
deschoolers in society in general. The first calls for
the abolition of compulsory schooling to free men,
the second calls for the strengthening of schools so
that they can resist society's pressures. The progressives start from a concept of individuality derived
from the Romantic Movement. The extreme
progressive viewpoint is ultimately a call for
'communitas' and is non-rational. In practice the
progressives have all been moderates asking for a
'contract community' in which individuals have the
right to act as equals and have an equal right to break
the social contract if they do not feel it is any longer
in their interests. Their arguments have been for an
egalitarian comprehensive ideology which implies
equality of opportunity. Equality of opportunity is
an idea which brings together both individual
development and societal judgment of that development. The problem for the supporters of an
egalitarian comprehensive ideology has been therefore
that of deciding when to allow individual freedom of
development and when to allow societal judgment.
Like the moderate deschools they see the autonomy
of the school as a means of staving off societal pressures.

Chapter 5

The Reality of
Hierarchy

The concept of hierarchy implies three things. First
it implies categorisation; second it implies that the
categories that are distinguished will be differentially
evaluated and, third it implies a relative stability to
the categorisation and evaluation. Hierarchy can be
seen therefore as the recognition and evaluation of
differences so as to form a relatively stable structure.
The education system can be seen as such a complex
hierarchical structure. It can be visualised as a ball of
knotted strings. Each length of string can be
analytically separated out to represent a hierarchic
ordering. It is the ball of string which is the reality
however and to separate out each length that com-
poses the ball is to lose that reality. Yet to understand
the ball it is necessary to trace each piece of string
and to see it in relation to all the other pieces of
string. This would be a difficult enough task if it was
a ball of string that had to be explained. When the
pieces of string are themselves abstractions called
hierarchies the task is even more difficult, for as soon

as the decision is taken to separate out one hierarchic ordering, e.g. a hierarchy of schools, it becomes obvious that the ranking of schools cannot be explained without also discussing the ranking of pupils, teachers and knowledge, for those three items comprise the elements with which a school can be described and ranked, e.g. a school for pupils whose parents are of a high social class is more highly regarded than a school which teaches pupils of low social class. On the other hand a ranking of any of the three elements of pupils, teachers and knowledge is itself dependent upon a ranking of schools, e.g. a grammar schoolboy is more highly ranked than a secondary modern schoolboy regardless of his social origins. Similar relationships between rankings of teachers or rankings of knowledge and ranking of schools could also be demonstrated. This is not the limit of the complexities involved however. To explain these further complexities requires a simple chart (see Table 4) on which the main elements involved in creating hierarchic orderings are set out. It will be the task of the remainder of this chapter to explicate this chart.

Table 4   The elements of hierarchic ordering

	Schools (which are themselves ranked)		
	Pupils	*Teachers*	*Knowledge*
Categories of evaluation	Age Sex Academic ability Social class	Age (experience) Sex Academic ability Social class Administrative position	Abstraction Assessment Literacy Individualisation

Even with the aid of this chart the full complexity of the entangled ball of string is still not evident. What has to be realized is that each of the criteria of evaluation is itself compounded both across the chart horizontally — so that, for example, older pupils are usually taught by male teachers who use higher levels of abstraction — and also vertically — so that pupils over sixteen years of age are more likely to be male, of higher academic ability and higher social class — and both horizontal and vertical criteria are also compounded such that pupils in the sixth form are likely to be predominantly male, of higher social class and ability and to be taught abstract, individualised, literate knowledge for formal assessment by experienced male teachers of high academic ability, high social class and holding a high administrative position.

There are thus three elements that constitute a school that can be analytically distinguished, although in any empirical situation they are inextricably compounded; they are pupils, teachers and knowledge. The result of their compounded hierarchies is a hierarchy which typifies an individual school and gives it its uniqueness, for each individual school has a different admixture of these three hierarchical elements and it is by this admixture that the school is itself ranked in relation to other schools. This compound nature of the school as a hierarchical organisation presents very difficult problems of explanation because, although it is possible to conceive of hierarchies of knowledge separate from hierarchies of pupils and hierarchies of teachers, any explanation of any one hierarchy rests in part at least on reference to one or more of the other hierarchies, e.g. one of the hierarchic orderings of teachers can be indicated only by referring to the subjects (i.e. knowledge) they teach. The procedure that has been followed in this chapter is to start with an historical explanation of the hierarchies of knowledge because such an explanation does not have to be validated by reference to either a pupil or teacher hierarchy. The various pupil hierarchies are then described referring to knowledge hierarchies where necessary. Finally, hierarchies of teachers are discussed referring to hierarchies of knowledge and hierarchies of pupils when these hierarchies demonstrate teacher hierarchies. In this way the complexity of the empirical situation can be gradually built up without forcing the reader to take on trust hierarchic orderings that are to be explained later. It has to be realised however that this is simply a device for explanation. It would have been equally valid to start with hierarchies of teachers and work in the opposite direction — the reality is the entangled ball of string not the individual pieces of string that comprise it.

Hierarchies of Knowledge

A hierarchy requires first that there be units differentiated from each other which can be ranked in order, and so any explanation of such a hierarchy requires an explanation of the differentiation and specialisation of knowledge into discrete units. This

differentiation was a product of the late nineteenth
century.

The creation of hierarchical and differentiated
units of knowledge was evident initially in post-
revolutionary France. The Napoleonic reforms of the
education system made education the servant of the
state and the French universities were, and are,
institutions in which the individual could be trained
in accomplishments useful to the state. The most
useful accomplishment in a Napoleonic army was that
of engineering and thus engineering became and
remains the highest status subject in the education
system. The French state was committed to a policy
of equality and so it had to find some means to
select those who were to qualify which did not rely
on personal preference or aristocratic birth. At the
same time such a system of selection had to remain
under state control for education existed for the state.
The solution arrived at was to prescribe the
curriculum and institute an examination, also
controlled by the state, of candidates for professional
positions. High status knowledge in France therefore
became knowledge that was formally assessed (for a
discussion of the French educational tradition see
Vaughan 1969).

The success of the French universities was influen-
tial in the shape that the German universities took in
the late nineteenth century. The German universities
(the following discussion of German universities relies
on the account of Ben-David and Zloczower 1962),
like their French predecessors, were controlled by the
state. However unlike the French universities the

German universities did not have their curriculum prescribed. In Germany only the final professional examinations were set by the state. This meant that the universities were free to act as they saw fit as long as the students were prepared for the state examination. To mark their separation from the state examinations, which were concerned with the practical aspects of a profession, the university staffs emphasised the theoretical aspects of a profession. Knowledge which was abstracted and unrelated to everyday life was thus highly valued, for by producing such knowledge the universities asserted their independence of the state. As well as the creation of a hierarchy of knowledge in which abstract knowledge is more highly valued than practical knowledge, German universities can also be credited with creating the specialist subject or discipline independent of any profession or practical utility. The creation was an accident of their academic hierarchy. In the German university the professor was, and is, a god-like figure who rules his department absolutely — he dictates his subordinates' teaching duties and his subordinates' research. It was therefore highly desirable to be a professor. A professor, however, was a man who had mastered his subject completely. To become a professor meant that one had to wait for the death of an existing incumbent or create a new subject. Enterprising and ambitious men soon realised that to become a professor meant working on the fringes of the subject they had been taught until it could be called a separate subject worthy of a chair. Hence the creation of numerous specialist subjects.

By the turn of the century the success of the
German universities in producing scholars meant that
just as they modelled themselves on the successful
French so they became the model for British and
American universities and so to some extent there was
the growth in England of subjects, theoretical
knowledge (which implies research) and formal
assessment, particularly in the new civic universities.
However Germany and America were both federal in
structure and had a large number of universities
competing with one another for eminence — each
state in the USA and each *land* in Germany seeking to
outdo its rival. England had only a few universities and
there was little doubt that the eminent universities
were Oxford and Cambridge. Oxford and Cambridge
were both committed to teaching rather than research
and to the ideal of the pious gentleman: their concern
was with producing gentlemen by communal living
not researchers in more and more specialist subjects.
Even today they pride themselves on producing
generalists rather than specialists. The result of the
graft of the German ideas of specialisation and
abstraction on to the English ideal of a cultured
gentleman was a mongrel; subjects, specialisation and
research all began to intrude but the abstraction of
knowledge, which had been in Germany a defence
against the state's intrusion into the university,
became in England an argument for maintaining
the vocationally irrelevant and abstract subjects
associated with the life of a gentleman — the classical
curriculum — at the top of the hierarchy of knowledge.
Engineers, the élite in France, and chemists, the élite

in Germany, were given very low status in English
university life. Although today the Arts curriculum
has largely supplanted the classical curriculum, the
inferior status of science, particularly applied science,
remains a feature of the academic hierarchy.

The creation of specialisation, and formal examinations was not however solely a product of the French
and German educational systems. It was also a
product of the changes that were occurring in society
in the nineteenth century. Societal changes and
educational changes are related, for education systems
do not exist separate from the societies of which they
form a part. Two related changes in European society
are associated with specialisation and formal assessment. There was first the increasing industrialisation
and second the increasing bureaucratisation of
society. Industrialisation produced an increasing
specialisation and division of the work force. A
differentiated work force required differentiated
training in the education system and this the education system was able to provide by the specialisation
of knowledge. Industrialisation was also associated
with bureaucratisation for as organisations grew
larger and larger there arose a greater need for some
structured form of co-ordination. This was provided
by bureaucratic administrative structures. The state
also adopted bureaucratic structures to enable it to
regulate and control the lives of its citizens. Bureaucratic structures demand formal records of decisions
taken and thus require of their members literacy.
They demand of the individual that he be an individual
unit, not one of a family or a group, because the ties

he has outside his office are not allowed to intrude into his office work. At the same time as these developments of industrialisation and bureaucratisation were occurring, there was an ideological commitment to the ethic of individual self-sufficiency, and competition amongst individuals was seen as leading to the benefit of society. The result of these pressures was that, as a contemporary observer (Weber 1948, p.240) pointed out,

> educational institutions on the European continent, especially the institutions of higher learning . . . are dominated and influenced by the need for the kind of 'education' that produces a system of specialised examinations and the trained expertness that is increasingly indispensable for modern bureaucracy.

The arguments above suggest that as society began to differentiate and rank occupations so too was knowledge differentiated and ranked. It was differentiated and ranked in such a way (see Young 1971) that

(a)   abstract knowledge, knowledge unrelated to everyday life, is more highly valued than practical knowledge — a legacy of the German universities;

(b)   knowledge that is formally assessed is more highly valued than knowledge that is not assessed — a legacy of the French impetus for equality and the bureaucratisation of society;

(c)   knowledge based on literacy is more highly valued than that based on manual skills or oracy — a legacy of bureaucratisation, and

(d)   individualised knowledge is more highly valued
        than communal knowledge — a product of
        literacy, bureaucracy, industrialisation and the
        ideology of individual competition.

The relationship between the differentiation and
evaluation of occupations and the differentiation and
ranking of knowledge was thus not a simple one of
cause and effect. It was mediated by different
structures of higher education in different countries,
differential control by the state over higher education
and different cultural ideals of the educated man.

Hierarchies of Pupils

Pupils are categorised within, and between, schools
in terms of their academic ability, their sex, their age
and their social class. The first of these categories,
that of academic ability, it is the expressed function
of schools to recognise, develop and evaluate. The
other three categories are socially recognised to
varying degrees in different schools but are not the
central concern of schools, being societal categories
which the school may or may not recognise. The
ideology of equality of opportunity is particularly
concerned with avoiding the compounding of the
ability hierarchy with the other hierarchies of age,
sex and, especially, social class.

    The ranking of pupils in terms of some criterion
of ability is a feature of most English secondary
schools (see Table 5).

Table 5   Ability specialisation by grouping

(A) *Scale of ability specialisation*

  0   non streaming
  1   non streaming with separate remedial group
  2   non streaming with setting
  3   banding (each stream contains more than one class
          group)
  4   streaming (with or without setting)

(a score of 0 on the scale means low ability specialisation, a
score of 4 high ability specialisation).

(B) *Mean score of ability specialisation*

	All secondary modern	*All comprehensive*	*All grammar*
Year	37	17	18
1	2·9	2·6	0·4
2	3·2	2·7	2·4
3	3·6	3·1	2·9
4	3·5	3·3	3·0

Source: Adapted from Tables 70 and 71 in King (1973).

The variations in ability differentiation in the
different types of school would suggest different
problems and different ideologies. The comprehensive
schools are particularly interesting because they were
set up with a rhetoric that espoused at the least
equitable treatment for all pupils and at the most
egalitarian treatment whereby aid should go
disproportionately to those in need. Both of these
ideologies are anti-hierarchical and yet the reality is a
stronger hierarchy than in the grammar schools,
although a weaker hierarchy than in the secondary
moderns. Three reasons can be given for this disparity

between the rhetoric of their founding ideologies and the reality of their practice. The first is that there is no disparity. Neither of the founding ideologies necessarily presuppose a lack of ability hierarchies. The equitable comprehensive ideology is part of a conception of the school that does not deny inequalities but only calls for equal treatment for all pupils, whilst the egalitarian ideology can be interpreted as an ideology of equality of opportunity and that ideology implies inequality. Nevertheless there is a tension between the ideologies and the practice because the egalitarian ideology stresses individuality over structure in its extreme form and the line is not clearly drawn between the extreme and moderate egalitarian positions. Both the moderate and the extreme egalitarians are concerned with developing the individual's potential, but the moderates want the child's academic potential to be fully developed whereas the extremists want the child's potential as an individual developed regardless of whether that potential demonstrates itself in academic or non-academic pursuits. A moderate stance values the child for his academic achievement and, although not inevitably, it follows that such valuation ranks children in terms of that achievement — it differentiates them by ability. The extreme egalitarian stance denies any structure and any ranking. The second reason for the disparity between ideology and practice, if disparity there be, lies in the wider ability intake of the comprehensive school. It is easier to deal with a mixed ability group of children if the abilities that are mixed are not that much different from each other, which is the situation in the grammar schools. The comprehensive schools take in a much wider ability range (in fact a full implementation of the comprehensive principle should mean comprehensive schools taking in the full ability range). Given this fact it is a measure of the power of the egalitarian ideology that comprehensive schools have a lower score on a scale of ability differentiation than secondary modern schools and that their most common mode of ability ranking is to use bands, i.e. to have groups of mixed ability within a limited ability range (see King 1973, Table 67) which is a less extreme form of ability differentiation than streaming. The third reason for a disparity between ideology and practice is related to societal pressures. Heads who may themselves be strong supporters of some form of egalitarian ideology practice rigorous selection so that their pupils may achieve examination success. They do this because they know that parents, employers, teachers and other headmasters judge a school as successful if its pupils perform well in external examinations. A.S. Neill may see the purpose of a school as that of promoting happiness, but parents want their children to be successful as well as happy and often equate the two aims.

The methods of allocating pupils into a niche in the ability hierarchy varies from school to school (and when the allocation by ability is between schools, from one local education authority to another). Some use standardised IQ tests, some teachers' reports and some internal examinations and some use various combinations of these methods. Whatever the method of allocation, however, the result is that pupils grouped together and classed as being of similar ability receive similar treatment. Teachers hold different expectations of pupils in different ability groups both in terms of their social and academic behaviour (see Hargreaves 1967, and Lacey 1970, for an extensive discussion of this aspect of ability grouping). This differential treatment is usually formalised with respect to academic behaviour by the 'less able' pupils being given differential access to knowledge; the different treatment in terms of social behaviour is more likely to be informal so that, for example, teachers finding a low ability pupil misbehaving are more likely to punish him than to punish a high ability pupil engaging in similar behaviour. The manner in which less able pupils are given differential access to knowledge is both by exclusion and inclusion. They are excluded from those aspects of knowledge which are abstract, formally assessed, based on literacy and individualised and are given greater periods of time on non-examination practical subjects requiring the use of the hands or the body. In any individual school this means less specialist science, less languages and more woodwork, technical drawing, physical education and domestic science (King 1973). The pupils do not always share the hierarchy of knowledge held by society (see Williams and Finch 1968) and 'able' pupils often complain at their exclusion from 'practical' subjects, but in societal terms it is the less able who are excluded not the able.

The differentiation of pupils into age groups and

the ranking of those groups so as to create hierarchies is a general feature of our society which is reflected in the organisation of schools: pupils are divided into infant, junior and secondary and although the age lines are not as clear and rigid as they once were there is little doubt that these divisions reflect a general ranking whereby the older the pupil the higher he is in the age hierarchy. Within secondary schools the same pattern of evaluation and hierarchy obtains. How far there is variation between different types of secondary schools, as there was for ability hierarchies, is difficult to ascertain for the empirical evidence (see King 1973) refers to age differentiation — i.e. the extent to which age is used as a criterion to differentiate pupils; it does not refer to the evaluation of these differentiated categories. However, if the presumption is made that differential treatment of older pupils is preferential treatment of older pupils, a reasonable assumption in our society, then it is clear that comprehensive schools have greater age hierarchies than either grammar or secondary modern schools (see Table 6). Even allowing for the lesser age range of pupils in secondary modern schools the evidence still suggests that comprehensive schools do have a greater age hierarchy. Just as ability, however measured, is used as a criterion for access to high status knowledge, so too is age: older pupils are given access to chemistry and physics rather than general science and are allowed to study more languages. With age another variable demonstrates the hierarchy clearly, that of expenditure. It is formally laid down that there is a higher per capita expenditure on older pupils, of

Table 6   Mean score of age specialisation

	All secondary modern	*All* comprehensive	*All* grammar
Number of schools	37	17	18
Mean	8·31	14·00	13·49

Source: Adapted from Table 93 in King (1973).

which one aspect is the lower pupil-teacher ratio. This variable is also evident in the hierarchy of ability although less obvious because it has been obscured by the division of pupils into two different types of school: secondary modern and grammar. Of these two types of school those for the less able, the secondary modern schools, receive lower per capita income and higher pupil-teacher ratios than grammar schools (Ross 1972). How far this is true of pupils of different abilities in comprehensive schools is even more difficult to ascertain, but Bates (1970) found little relationship between the proportion of less able pupils in schools and the number of allowances per pupil given to the schools, which would suggest that between comprehensive schools there is little disparity due to a higher proportion of less able pupils in one school rather than another.

Sex, like age, is socially recognised and evaluated so that men are more highly ranked than women. (The argument of 'Womens Lib' is that there is a difference which should be socially recognised but not evaluated.) In education the position is interesting because, although there are schools for different sexes, there

seems little evidence of a ranking of boys' schools
above girls' schools in the state system. In the private
sector, however, there remains a distinct divide and
discussion of 'the public schools' usually means
discussion of the public schools for boys with
interest and concern with girls coming, both
historically and today, as an afterthought. The
problem is, as it was with age, to distinguish differentiation of the sexes from hierarchical ranking. The
evidence, limited though it is, suggests that in mixed
schools the separation of the sexes — which is an
important feature of those schools in all aspects of
school life, with separate entrances for different sexes,
separation in school assembly and separate seating at
dinner — does not imply such a hierarchy (King 1973).
However when one looks at the relationship of the
sex hierarchy to the knowledge hierarchy it is obvious
that girls are more likely to be given less prestigeful
subjects of study, being restricted to subjects of a
similar nature to those being studied by low ability
pupils: practical, non-examinable and general rather
than specialist. The sex hierarchy is also compounded
with the age hierarchy in that the division of pupils
into single sex schools does not take place usually
until secondary education and sex differentiation in
mixed schools tends to vary with age with sixth
formers being allowed to mix much more freely (King
1973). The sex hierarchy can also be compounded
with the ability hierarchy in that girls are likely to be
over-represented in the top streams in primary schools
(Lunn 1970), although King (1973) found no
evidence of this over-representation in secondary

schools. In any empirical situation all the various
hierarchies can be compounded, e.g. only older girls
in top streams may be taught specialist science.

The full possibilities of compound pupil hierarchies
can only be demonstrated in their entirety when the
hierarchy of social class is added to the hierarchies of
knowledge, ability, age and sex which have already
been discussed. Because a concern with the egalitarian
comprehensive ideology implies that only ability
should be used as a criterion to rank pupils there has
been a plethora of research evidence that seeks to
demonstrate that other hierarchies than ability
intrude also into educational practice, particularly the
social class hierarchy. It is this evidence which can be
used here to demonstrate social class hierarchies of
pupils. There is now little doubt that pupils are ranked
in schools in terms of their social class although
teachers do not intentionally plan this. (For a
comprehensive list of the evidence for this statement
see UNESCO 1971.) The social class composition of a
school places it in a hierarchy in relation to other
schools just as a pupil's social class places him in a
hierarchy in relation to other pupils (Marceau 1975).
The reason for the higher position of higher class
pupils is that there is a relationship between the social
class of pupils and their school attainment. To
enumerate the possible causes of this relationship
would be to list most of the British work on the
sociology of education since 1945. (Banks, 1971,
provides such a summary.) However two themes can
be singled out. On the one hand are those researchers
who look for the cause in the lower class pupils'

inability to succeed at school. These either point
directly to the lower average intelligence score of the
lower class pupils on standardised scales (Crowther
1960, Douglas 1968), or to some aspect of their
upbringing such as their language (Bernstein 1958),
their parents' attitudes to education (Wiseman 1967)
or their inability to defer gratification in anticipation
of future rewards (Swift, 1966). On the other hand
are those researchers who see the cause lying in the
school system itself, either in the simple fact that
lower class pupils get poorer educational facilities
(Floud et al. 1957) or, more subtly, in the fact that
schools encourage and expect behaviour which is
more 'natural' to pupils from higher classes (Bernstein
1970, King 1969b). Wherever the cause of the
relationship between school attainment and social
class membership is located, the reality of the
relationship remains and produces a hierarchy of
pupils based on social class. The link between attainment and social class has led some researchers to
suggest that the formal organisation of ability in
schools, ability grouping, is directly related to social
class so that top streams contain a higher proportion
of higher class students than would be justified by
intelligence scores alone. Although this was found
to be the case when the institution of streaming was
looked at across many primary schools (Douglas 1968)
and was also found to be the case in a few secondary
schools selected for case study (Holly 1965, Ford
1969), it was not found to be a general feature of a
sample of secondary schools (see Table 7), although
it did occur in approximately 35 per cent of the

Table 7   Over-representation of non-manual[1] pupils in upper
            streams

	All secondary modern		All comprehensive		All grammar	
	Number of schools					
Year	(a)	(b)	(c)	(d)	(e)	(f)
	with over represen- tation	with streaming	with over represen- tation	with streaming	with over represen- tation	with streaming
2	3	12	1	1	1	1
4	4	10	3	7	1	6

Source: Unpublished data from the study reported in King (1973)
[1]The term non-manual, or its alternative middle class, is used to
refer to occupations I, II, IIIa in the Registrar-General's scale and
manual, or working class, refers to IIIb, IV, V on the same scale.
When used of pupils it refers to the fathers' occupation.

streamed schools and no instance was found of the
reverse situation, i.e. an over-representation of lower
class pupils in upper streams. Just as ability hierarchies
are compounded with social class hierarchies, so too are
sex, age and knowledge hierarchies. Girls are less likely
to continue in education than are boys but working class
girls are less likely than middle class girls (King 1971).
Older pupils are more likely to be middle class because
middle class pupils are successful at school. Coupled
with the fact that per capita expenditure on pupils is
related to age, this means that upper class boys receive
a disproportionate proportion of educational expenditure. Finally there is the compounding of the knowledge
and social class hierarchies; because lower class pupils are
more likely to be in lower streams, leave school early and

present problems of discipline they are often given access to knowledge of a non-specialist, practical kind. This special curriculum in which subjects as such are not taught is often given the title of the 'Newsom curriculum' after a report (Newsom 1963) which called for special treatment for pupils who were not benefiting from normal school subjects. The word often used for this curriculum is 'relevancy', and the educational idea is closely bound up with the concept of the community school discussed in an earlier chapter whereby pupils are taught using the local community as a source. The success of such a curriculum in engaging the interest of low stream, low social class pupils is difficult to evaluate. What it implies however is that for such pupils knowledge has to be limited both in abstraction and concomitant geographical location. The knowledge hierarchy is thus compounded with the age hierarchy, the ability hierarchy and the social class hierarchy. Even within the low status knowledge group of subjects there is some evidence of a further social class hierarchy (cited by Marceau 1975) whereby the lower the social class of a pupil the more likely he is to be trained in practical skills that are of little utility in finding a job.

Hierarchies of Teachers

Teachers can be ranked in terms of their age, their sex, their demonstrated academic ability, their social class of origin and the administrative position they hold in schools. Just as the various hierarchies of pupils are compounded with each other and with the knowledge hierarchies, so too are the various ways in which teachers are ranked compounded with each other, with the pupil hierarchies and with the knowledge hierarchies.

The hierarchy which is expressly recognised in the salary scale is that of age. Strictly, annual increments of salary are given for teaching experience, but mature entrants to teaching usually receive more than the basic starting salary so some allowance is made for age and for the majority of teachers age is closely correlated with experience of teaching. The age of the pupils taught by teachers is as important in their relative ranking as their own age. Those teaching pupils in secondary schools have much more chance of a 'graded post', i.e. a position in the educational system which carries with it both responsibility and extra salary. In addition those teaching older pupils are more likely to be subject specialists rather than general teachers, and the higher evaluation of specialisms in the knowledge hierarchy means a higher evaluation of those teaching them.

Sex, since the introduction of equal pay for women, is no longer as clear a hierarchical division as it once was amongst teachers. However it remains important because women teachers are less likely than men to achieve promotion, because so many are expected to break their careers to look after children. It is also important because women teachers are much more numerous in the teaching of the lower age range of pupils, there are few male infant teachers for example, and the low status of their pupils means that

women too have low status. The predominance of
women in primary teaching implies also a link
between sex and low status, generalist knowledge in
that primary schools teach knowledge that has a
lower status. The concentration of new pedagogical
methods in primary education may stem, in part at
least, from a desire to erect a new hierarchy of professional pedagogy as a counter-weight to the general
societal devaluing of primary education because of
the low status of the knowledge transmitted in it.

Perhaps one of the most important hierarchies of
teachers, as it is for pupils, is that of academic ability.
Just as the pupils are divided into academic ranks
based upon some past measure of academic achievement so too are the staff. Two strands of this
academic ordering can be distinguished. The first is
concerned with the type of academic qualification
achieved: teachers with university degrees are more
highly rated than those without degrees. Further
subtle distinctions are made within the category of
teachers with degrees: those with higher degree
classifications and those with degrees from Oxford
and Cambridge being given a higher status position
than the other degree holders. These distinctions are
very important not only in terms of status but also
in terms of salary and promotion. In terms of salary
graduates get more than non-graduates and those with
'seconds' or 'firsts' get more than other graduates;
with respect to promotion it is rare for a non-graduate
to become a head of a secondary school. (The
compounding of hierarchies is demonstrated here in
that non-graduates often become heads of primary

schools.) The second strand of academic ordering is concerned with the subject taught. Obviously this strand is linked with the first because some subjects, such as physical education or domestic science, are not taught to degree level or are taught to such a level at only a few universities. However it can be distinguished from the first as more directly linked to the knowledge hierarchy. The distinction between degree and non-degree is also linked to the knowledge hierarchy in that degree level work is presumed to be more abstract than non-degree level work. Where subject is concerned the link is direct — the more abstract, literate and individualised a subject the higher its status, and the higher the status of the teacher teaching it. To leave the discussion of the compounding of the knowledge hierarchy and the teacher hierarchy here would be to oversimplify the picture. Although it is generally true that abstract subjects have higher status than practical subjects in schools distinctions are also made between abstract subjects. These vary historically so that a teacher teaching religious knowledge today will probably have lower status in a school than a maths teacher, even if he has a degree and the maths teacher has not, although fifty years ago the teacher of religious knowledge would probably have been more highly placed. The pre-eminence of English and mathematics throughout the historical development of the English school is because these abstract subjects provide the basic skills necessary for life in our industrial society.

A good example of the present day hierarchic ordering of subjects is presented in the study of

'Hightown Grammar' undertaken by Colin Lacey
(1970). He presents a detailed picture of the
academic hierarchy by listing the various
responsibility allowances in the school he studied
(see Table 8).

Table 8   Responsibility allowances in 'Hightown Grammar'

Cash allowances per annum £	Heads of department	Deputy heads of department	Others
450	English, maths	—	—
355	History, geography, French, chemistry	—	—
260	Biology, physics	—	—
165	Art, music, handicrafts	English, history, French, maths	—
100	Physical education, economics	Geography	English, chemistry, physics, biology, physical education

Source: Lacey (1970).

This distribution of allowances is confirmed in Bates's (1970)
study of fifty comprehensive schools with 50 per cent of
responsibility allowances going to academic subjects and only
27 per cent to other subjects (the remainder going to remedial
and pastoral care posts).

The evidence for teachers being ranked in terms of
past academic achievement is so profuse as to almost
pass unnoticed because the hierarchy is so much a
part of the conception of the school. Evidence for a
hierarchy of social class is much more difficult to
find. There is certainly evidence, cited above, that
teachers who teach pupils of higher social class have
a higher position in any ranking because of the
relationship between social class and academic
attainment. Evidence on the social class origins of
teachers is, however, much more difficult to obtain.
That such a hierarchy exists was demonstrated by
Floud and Scott (1961) who showed that the higher
the social class composition of the pupils in a school
the higher the social class composition of the teaching
staff. How far this correlation occurs within schools
has not however been subject to empirical test, so
although it may be postulated that high social class
origins lead to high positions in a hierarchy of
teachers there is no evidence, as yet, to confirm or
deny the hypothesis.

The final hierarchic ordering of teachers to be
discussed is the one most directly associated with
power. Schools are organisations and like all
organisations have to be co-ordinated. This
co-ordination is achieved in schools by the creation
of an administrative hierarchy in which each occupant
of a position in the hierarchy is given control over
aspects of a school's functioning with, in English
schools, overall administrative control being granted
to the head. This hierarchy is compounded with all
the other teacher hierarchies with positions of control

going to older male teachers with good degrees
teaching academic subjects (and coming from high
social classes?). A complicating factor in this picture
is provided by the growth of large comprehensive
schools. First, as was pointed out in Chapter 2, they
create yet another hierarchy of teachers — one based
on pastoral care. There is some evidence that this
hierarchy provides an alternative career structure for
teachers who would not be given administrative
positions normally because they teach non-academic
subjects or they are responsible for too few pupils or
they do not have degrees (Mays et al. 1968), e.g. in
'Hightown Grammar' (Lacey 1970) of four heads of
houses, two were deputy heads of English and history
departments respectively but of the other two heads
of house one was head of Latin, a declining subject,
and one was head of handicrafts, a practical subject.
Second there is the suggestion that a different
administrative structure will be created in such large
schools. This has already been touched upon when
discussing the possibility of a devolution of power
from the 'sovereign head'. It is raised again here
because any change in the administrative hierarchy in
such schools would imply a change in the hierarchies
of teachers. There is no doubt that comprehensive
schools are generally larger (see Table 9) and more
complex than other secondary schools, both because
of the wider ability range of their pupils and because
of the larger number of subjects taught in such
schools (see Table 10). The problem is one of
deciding how far such size and complexity affects the
administrative hierarchy.

Table 9   Number of secondary schools by size and status

| | Number of pupils | | | |
	0-799	800-1,499	1,500+	Total
Comprehensive	835	657	99	1,591
Secondary modern	2,033	183	2	2,218
Grammar	722	120	1	893

Source: HMSO, *Statistics of Education for England and Wales*, vol. 1, 1972.

Table 10   Mean number of subjects taught

	Comprehensive Schools	Secondary Modern Schools	Grammar Schools
No. of schools	17	37	18
Mean	28·1	18·8	21·7

Source: Adapted from Table 51, King (1973).

Evidence from an intensive study of a grammar school, a secondary modern school and a comprehensive school supplemented by a more superficial study of eighty secondary schools of varying size and status suggests that there is an effect (Easthope 1973). The effect is not however a devolution of power from the head but the creation of a new structure on which the middle levels in the administrative hierarchy gain power at the expense of the lower levels (see Table 11). What this means is that senior staff and heads of department in the comprehensive school had more power than their counterparts in the smaller secondary modern school and grammar school and that assistant teachers in the comprehensive school had less power than their counterparts in the secondary modern school and grammar school.

This suggestion of a more hierarchical pattern of administrative control in the comprehensive was supported by other evidence. First, when the teachers were asked to list the staff who were very important to them every day the assistant teachers in the comprehensive school were much more likely to specify their head of department than their counterparts in the other two schools and much less likely to specify the headteacher. Second it was also supported by an examination of the staff handbook, a feature of the comprehensive school, which contained explicit statements specifying hierarchical channels of communication and spheres of power and responsibility:

It is his [head of department's] responsibility to report to the head master any difficulty.

Subject teachers should look to their head of department for clear guidance.

Requisition forms must bear the signature of the head of department even though some orders may originate from other members of that department.

Table 11 Standardised[1] power scores[2] in schools of different status

	Comprehensive					Secondary Modern					Grammar				
	Head	Senior staff	Heads of department	Assistant teachers	Heads of house	Head	Senior staff	Heads of department	Assistant teachers	Heads of house	Head	Senior staff	Heads of department	Assistant teachers	Heads of house
Power as[3] perceived by head	59	23	9	4	7	55	9	7	8	14	42	9	7	24	5
Power as[3] perceived by deputy head	41	41	20	4	13	60	33	11	14	17	13	15	13	30	16
Power as[4] perceived by all staff	13	12	17	5	1	16	8	13	7	0	15	4	15	7	1

1 The standardisation of the scores means they can be compared between schools. Such a comparison leads to the conclusions given in the text.

2 The concept of power used is not a zero sum concept of power, thus increasing power for the middle levels of staff does not *imply* decreasing power for the heads or assistant teachers.

3 Derived by listing all situations in a school and asking for each aspect of that situation: who decided (power), was consulted (influence), or had to approve a decision (authority), e.g. who decides, who is consulted, whose approval is needed before a decision is taken on whether teaching should occur, who should be taught, who should teach, what textbooks and equipment were to be used, where it should occur, when and for how long it should occur, what should be taught and how it should be taught. The score was calculated using the formula:

$$C = \frac{c}{T} \times 100$$

where
C = a person or a group's score
c = the number of acts of control (power or authority or influence) undertaken by that person or group
T = total number of acts of control for an aspect.

4 This was derived by asking all teachers who had a say in various situations and how much say these people had. The method is described in Tannenbaum 1956, 1961, 1962.

Third the sample of eighty schools provided further evidence of hierarchy when a content analysis of documents returned by twenty-nine schools demonstrated that the comprehensive schools which returned documents had a higher specification of the role of their middle level staff, with respect to the administrative aspects of that role, than the grammar or secondary modern schools who also returned documents. (This conclusion has to be treated with caution because of the small number of schools returning documents, none the less it does lend support to the more detailed study discussed above.)

Conclusion

An examination of knowledge, pupils and teachers demonstrates therefore a picture of hierarchies, hierarchies which are complex and compounded. This is not however the end of the pattern of hierarchy in English education. Two further hierarchies can be distinguished. The first is the hierarchy between schools which is closely related to the three patterns of hierarchies already discussed. Briefly, as was pointed out in the previous chapter, it has been demonstrated in a succession of empirical works that the separation of pupils into grammar and secondary modern schools leads to inequities (for a good summary of the evidence see Griffiths 1971). The inequities can be summarised as first inequities of selection and second inequities of resources. The selection process is inequitous because a pupil's chance of selection to a grammar school varies geographically (Taylor and Ayres 1969, Douglas 1968) and socially (Floud et al. 1957). The allocation of resources is inequitous because grammar schools receive more expenditure per capita and more favourable pupil-teacher ratios (Ross 1972). The creation of comprehensive schools does not remove any of these inequities between schools but merely places them in a new context. The ranking of schools is no longer related to their title, as grammar and secondary modern, but schools may still have intakes which are socially selective because of the differential location of social classes in different areas of a city and the differential esteem and resources given to secondary education in different local authority areas. The allocation of resources may also be inequitous from a national viewpoint because different local authorities allocate their resources differently. The various attempts to solve some of the social and geographical inequities within a locality, such as the creation of 'balanced catchment areas' and 'busing', have already been touched upon in the previous chapter so need not be laboured here except to point out that such policies are themselves regionally specific, and so do nothing to remove inequities between regions. The second hierarchy is even more fundamental than the hierarchy between schools. It is the hierarchy between teacher and pupil. This hierarchy has, like the hierarchy between schools, been discussed in the previous chapter where it was pointed out that the extreme progressive ideology calls for the abolition of this hierarchy.

There seems little empirical evidence of any response to this call in state secondary schools. The hierarchy is itself a compound of three analytically separate hierarchies: the hierarchy between adult and child, the hierarchy between the person responsible for order in an organisation and those under him (whether this is conceived of in bureaucratic or military terms) and the hierarchy between the knowledgeable and the ignorant. The extreme progressive ideology, as practised and preached by A.S. Neill, attacks the latter two hierarchies leaving order to be maintained communally and denying a concept of knowledge which would allow of hierarchy. Empirical studies of the hierarchy, of which the most famous is Waller's (1932) and one of the most recent is Lacey's (1970), point to the maintenance of social distance as the device whereby hierarchy is maintained. This is achieved in a variety of ways, e.g. special forms of address from pupil to teacher, pupils rising when a teacher enters a room, separate entrances for teachers, separate toilets, separate dining areas, special clothing (the gown), the maintenance of a 'teacher-face' when dealing with pupils, the use of special language forms to impart knowledge, etc. An attempt to measure this social distance (King 1973) using a selection of items found that four of these items were scalable and could be used to distinguish between schools (see Table 12). The results demonstrate the reality of the hierarchy between teacher and pupil, in all types of secondary school, with comprehensive schools demonstrating the least social distance and grammar the most.

The final conclusion that can be drawn therefore is that the educational system is a complex hierarchy in which hierarchies of knowledge, pupils, teachers and schools are mutually supporting and interlinked.

Table 12   Pupil-teacher differentiation

(A)   Scale of pupil-teacher differentiation

Item	Frequency
Teachers have special corridors or stairs	25
Teachers have different dining style	27
Teachers have special dining area	54
Teachers have special dining tables	64

(mean item analysis value 0·928, mean score 2·36, $n = 72$, SD = 1·10)

(B)   Mean score of pupil-teacher differentiation

	All comprehensive	All secondary modern	All grammar
No. of schools	17	37	18
Mean	1·65	2·46	2·83
Standard deviation	1·13	1·08	0·69

Source: Adapted from Tables 96 and 97 in King (1973).

Knowledge is categorised and the categories evaluated in such a way that high status knowledge is

individualised, literate, abstract and formally assessed.
Pupils are ranked so that able, older boys of high
social class occupy the higher ranks. Teachers are
hierarchically ordered so that those who possess high
status knowledge, are older, male, of high social class
and gain administrative responsibility occupy high
positions in the hierarchy. Schools are also hierarchically ordered in terms of the knowledge they transmit,
the pupils they teach and the teachers who comprise
their staffs and within schools there is a fundamental
hierarchy between teachers and pupils. In short the
social organisation of education implies categorisation
and evaluation; English schools are 'hierarchical
communities'.

Part 3

Open Education

Chapter 6

Open Education

It has been argued that the English school is characterised by hierarchies which are interlocked to form a 'hierarchical community' and that there are ideologies based on equity and ideologies based on egalitarianism which attack such a hierarchical conception of education. The equitable arguments call for equal treatment for all pupils (the equitable comprehensive ideology), or all teachers (the professional ideology) and as such may attack the conception of the school as a 'hierarchical community'.

A more fundamental attack however arises from the egalitarian ideologies whether progressive or deschooling. Both assert the primacy of the individual over the society and consequently attack not only hierarchies but all structures. The assertion of individual judgment over societal judgment of what counts as valid knowledge is a feature of both ideologies. This means that both deny social structuring of knowledge, for the only valid

structuring is that undertaken by the individual and
each individual will structure knowledge differently.
The societal differentiation of knowledge into discrete
bounded areas is consequently seen as illegitimate and
knowledge is perceived as 'integrated', the integration
being achieved by each individual. The primacy of
individual judgment of the importance of knowledge
areas necessitates not only a transcendence of the
boundaries of knowledge areas but also a
transcendence of the boundary between teacher and
pupil; if the sole judge of the importance of
knowledge is the individual then the teacher learns
along with his pupil because until the pupil indicates
which areas of knowledge are important to him the
teacher is powerless and unable to provide the
appropriate materials, skills or information. Both
ideologies also imply the transcendence of the
boundaries of the school. The deschooling ideology
takes this as its major emphasis but it is also a feature
of the progressive ideology with its stress upon the
natural child constrained by the artificial organisation
of society. In short, both ideologies call for the
abolition of structures and the transcendence of
boundaries to lead to an education that is
spontaneous, open and centred on the individual.

The progressive ideology has largely been used to
justify claims for the introduction of open education
in primary schools where such education is usually
termed 'the integrated day' or simply 'progressive
primary education'. (Empirical measures of open
education in primary education have been developed
and used to compare 'traditional' and 'progressive'

schools, see Traub et al., 1972, and Walberg and Thomas, 1972.) The deschooling ideology has largely been used to justify claims for the introduction of 'integrated curriculums' or 'open education' in secondary schools and, although proponents of open education in secondary schools recognise similarities between deschooling and progressive ideas, they rest their case on the deschooling ideology (e.g. see Richmond 1973). The reason for the different ideologies calling for similar ends attracting differential support in primary and secondary schools' education is not difficult to see. The problem in primary, and particularly infant, education is to harness the energy and enthusiasm, which is maverick in its interests and in the connections that young children make between areas of knowledge. Given this problem the progressive ideology provides a legitimation for a form of teaching that uses rather than suppresses 'natural' energy. The problem in secondary education is that of the bored and uninterested pupil. For this situation the deschooling ideology provides an explanation, the alienation of knowledge, and a solution that is similar to that provided by progressive education, namely to bring knowledge production back under the control of the individual so that it is relevant to him. Primary school children find relevancy and interest everywhere so school knowledge boundaries are ignored; secondary school children find school knowledge irrelevant there-fore knowledge boundaries are ignored to reach relevance.

Theoretical discussion of the move toward open education has seen it as a move (a) from closed

bounded structures of teachers, pupils and knowledge
to open boundary transcending situations and (b) as a
move from mechanical to organic solidarity. It is true
that the move to open education implies the
transcendence of boundaries. It is not true that it is a
move from mechanical to organic solidarity. The
concept of boundary transcendence is developed by
Bernstein from an initial formulation which merely
states that definitions of roles, groups, subject
boundaries and relationships with the outside are
implicit and blurred (Bernstein 1967) into a detailed
discussion of two concepts which he calls
'classification' and 'frame'. He says classification
'refers to the nature of the differentiation between
contents. Where classification is strong, contents are
well insulated from each other by strong boundaries'
(p. 49) and 'frame refers to the degree of control
teacher and pupil possess over the selection,
organisation and pacing of the knowledge transmitted
and received' (p. 50). Classification is concerned with
the boundaries of the curriculum, the 'contents', and
frame is concerned with the control teacher and pupil
have over the transmission of the contents, the
pedagogy. He then goes on to argue that open
education, which he calls an 'integrated code', is
characterised by weak classification and weak framing
while traditional education, which he calls 'collection
code', is characterised by strong classification and
strong framing. He adds therefore to the concept of
open education the idea that it can be characterised
not only by boundary transcendence of knowledge
areas, 'weak classification', but also by weak control

of teachers over the pedagogy, 'weak framing'. This weak framing is implied in the progressive and deschooling ideologies. They insist on strong control by the pupil, the individual learner, over the transmission of knowledge. It can be observed that where open education has been introduced teachers lose control of the pedagogy. Musgrove (1973) has

Table 13   Summary of the distinctions made in Chapter 1 between types of social order

Type of order	Relationship of areas of society to each other	Stability of areas	Reaction to individual and society	Order maintained by
Mechanical solidarity	Independent	Stable	Celebrates society	Allegiance to unquestioned values
Hierarchical community	Inter-dependent	Stable	Celebrates society	Allegiance to unquestioned values
Contract community	Inter-dependent	Stable	Celebrates individuality	Commitment to an ideology
Organic solidarity	Inter-dependent	Stable	Celebrates individuality	Commitment to 'collective consciousness'
Commun-itas	Inter-dependent	Unstable	Celebrates individuality	Commitment to a goal

argued against open education for this reason. It deprives teachers of the power given to them by their subject expertise and, he argues, leads that power to be given up to the head. Bernstein too sees this possibility but also points out that teachers may also give up their control of the pedagogy to an ideology, which decides for them the pedagogy that is to be followed.

In terms of the distinctions made in the first chapter of this book between types of social order (for a summary of which see Table 13), it is suggested that open education can be either a move to a 'contract community', in which the overarching ideology is equivalent to Durkheim's 'collective consciousness' (this conception of the overarching ideology as the 'collective consciousness' does not appear to have been made by Bernstein who sees it as paradoxical that there should be organic solidarity and an explicit ideology), or as a move to 'communitas', in which the individual pupil is the only one able to judge the validity and relevance of knowledge. By distinguishing in this manner between a move toward a 'contract community' and a move toward a 'communitas', rather than seeing open education solely as a move toward organic solidarity as Bernstein does, it is possible to distinguish between the different proponents of open education. The moderate deschoolers and progressives ask for a movement toward a 'contract community' in which there is a celebration of individuality within the stable structure of the school. The extreme deschoolers and progressives ask for a movement toward 'communitas' in which there is a celebration of individuality and spontaneity and a rejection of structure. Using the distinctions made in the first chapter between the two types of order that celebrate society, mechanical solidarity and 'hierarchical community' (see Table 13), enables further clarification and extension of Bernstein's analysis. Bernstein sees the move to open education as a move from mechanical solidarity to organic solidarity. He argues that the 'collection code', the traditional education, is a case of mechanical solidarity and the 'integrated code', open education, is a case of organic solidarity. He argues this because in the collection code group membership is unchanging and values are unquestioned and in the integrated code individuality is celebrated and there are no common experiences. It has already been pointed out above that open education may imply either organic solidarity or 'communitas' and that Bernstein does not distinguish between them. It is important to point out also that there is a difference between mechanical solidarity and 'hierarchical community' which is not made by Bernstein. With both mechanical solidarity and 'hierarchical community' there is a stress on the importance of the society over the individual, a stress upon unquestioned traditional values and the assertion of a stable structure. However the 'hierarchical community' differs from mechanical solidarity in that the social units within such a community are interdependent not independent. It is thus possible to have both specialised units and an organisational form similar to mechanical solidarity. The English school is a 'hierarchical community' and the move toward open education is not a move from an organisation typified by mechanical solidarity but a move from an organisation that can be characterised as a 'hierarchical community'. (Bernstein's conception of the traditional school as being typified by mechanical solidarity leads him to see a paradox in the fact that a collection code has specialised and differentiated units which as an organisation typified by mechanical solidarity it should not have. The paradox is resolved once it is realised that the traditional school is a 'hierarchical community' not an organisation typified by organic solidarity.) Open education can be conceived of therefore as a move not from mechanical to organic solidarity but from 'hierarchical community' to either organic solidarity or 'communitas'.

Conclusion

The egalitarian ideologies imply 'communitas': they assert and celebrate individuality and call for the transcendence of boundaries. Within education the progressive ideology has been used to legitimate pressure for open education in primary schools and the deschooling ideology has been used to legitimate pressure for open education in secondary schools. Theoretically discussion of open education has added to the formulation of open education as boundary transcendence the idea that open education implies a diminution of the power of teachers over the pedagogical process, with control passing to pupils or to an overarching ideology. The move towards open education is best understood as a move from 'hierarchical community' to 'contract community' or 'communitas', not as a move from mechanical to organic solidarity. Moderate egalitarians ask for movement toward a 'contract community' and extreme egalitarians ask for movement toward 'communitas'.

Chapter 7

The Open School

Open education as espoused by the extreme progressive and extreme deschooling ideologies calls for 'communitas'. The difficulty is to conceive of a mode of operating education which would allow 'communitas'. New forms of social organisation have to be devised that approximate 'communitas'. What form will these organisations take? What evidence is there of support for such organisations and what resistance is there to them? What would be the problems of a 'communitas' organisation? Tentative answers to these questions form the content of this chapter.

The situation at present is that the schools which espouse the egalitarian ideology, the comprehensive schools, far from setting up new forms of organisation and social order are adapting to the school the old organisational form of bureaucracy. They are intent upon this tack because the decision makers in those schools saw their increased size and complexity as a problem of control and co-ordination. Bureaucratic organisations are hierarchical and so the bureaucratic solution is isomorphous with the hierarchical conception of education. Such a solution is therefore not acceptable to those who support one of the anti-hierarchical ideologies. These supporters must therefore seek a form of organisation that solves the problems of control and co-ordination, in a manner which does not imply hierarchies. Such an organisation has been described in sociological literature both in the discussion of society in general and in the discussion of organisations. It appears under the titles of 'organic co-ordination' (Burns and Stalker 1961), 'post-administrative society' (Bennis 1971 and Willener 1965) and 'the adaptive learning system' (Schon 1973). Hage, Aiken and Marrett (1971) present the most succinct distinction between the two modes of achieving co-ordination, which they call 'programming' and 'feedback'. Programming refers to the specification of tasks by superiors in a hierarchy, a bureaucratic structure, and feedback refers to a process of continuous mutual adjustment by flows of information. They postulate that there are causal links between the diversification of an organisation, the volume of communication and the pattern of power. They argue that diversification will of necessity lead to increased communication to achieve co-ordination, but that this communication can be inhibited if there is already in existence a hierarchical structure of power. Much empirical work (see for example Katz and Kahn 1966) has demonstrated that

hierarchies inhibit the flow of information upward,
however well meaning those in positions of power are
about the free flow of information. The result where
there is already a hierarchical structure is therefore
likely to be programming rather than feedback, which
is the situation as it now exists in many schools.

To understand the distinctive features of a feedback organisational system it is necessary to look
closely at the descriptions of such a system given by
those arguing that this is a feature of post-industrial
society (Bennis 1971 and Willener 1965), at the
descriptions of those claiming to describe a new
organisational form (Schon 1973 and Burns and
Stalker 1961), and most importantly at the
descriptions of those who claim to see such a system
operating in education (Ben-David 1968, Richmond
1973) or wish to see such a system operating (Watts
1973, Armstrong 1973, Musgrove 1973).

The theorists who argue that the feedback system
will be a feature of post-industrial society point to
the accelerating pace of change as being one of the
major forces pushing organisations to devise new
systems of organisation to cope with a rapidly
changing unpredictable environment. The pre-
industrial organisation was based on the craft
principle: each craftsman was in control of the pace
at which he laboured, the length of time it took him
to complete a task, the tools he used to carry out the
task and the standard of workmanship that was
evidenced in the final production. The application of
rational principles to the process of production led to
its decline. The machine specified the workers' tasks,

the pace of the machine set the pace of the workman, his tools were provided by the machine and made to suit the machine rather than man. The whole process of production was divided into discrete units that were related to the machine rather than men. Thus although specialisation and assembly line working existed before machinery it was of a different order; it was a division into men's skills not a division into categories of work created by the manner in which a machine operated. Just as the 'rational' machine changed the tasks of the worker so 'rationality' was applied to administrative tasks to create the 'machine model' (Bennis 1971, p. 542) called bureaucracy. Bureaucracy was a great creative invention which served as a buffer against nepotism and partiality. It served also to bring about the demise of craftsmanship as an organising principle; the pace of work, the length of time needed to complete a task, the tools used for a task and the standards of workmanship were all decided outside the individual, who became in that telling phrase 'a cog in a machine'. Such a system was acceptable when change was comparatively slow, the environment was relatively stable and the hierarchical ordering of bureaucracy was in tune with a hierarchical ordering of society. Today, however, the environment is perceived to be more unpredictable and confused than formerly (how far the environment is more unpredictable than formerly and how far this is just a matter of perception is difficult to ascertain; whatever the true picture the result in terms of behaviour is the same). Organisations in a post-industrial society seek

therefore to limit the unpredictability of their
environment by bringing as much of their environment under control as possible. Thus industrial
organisations buy all aspects of a production process,
e.g. newspapers may seek to own chemical works and
engineering works to ensure supplies of ink and also
seek ownership of sawmills and forests to ensure
supplies of paper, while schools extend their influence
into the local area when they set themselves up as
community schools thus seeking control of some of
their external environment. As well as extending their
boundaries to encompass and control more of the
unpredictable environment, organisations may also
change themselves to produce a structure that can
cope with such an unpredictable environment.
Paradoxically it was the application of rationality to
the process of management that helped this process
of organisational change: rational theories of
decision-making encompass not only the internal
organisational forms but also the environment of the
organisation. To cope with an unpredictable
environment, decision taking structures had to be
created that were flexible enough to cope with that
unpredictability. These structures can be described as
a feedback organisational system.

Such structures, unlike bureaucracies, are in accord
with the anti-hierarchical theme prevalent in our
society. They can be characterised as 'adaptive
problem-solving, temporary systems of diverse
specialists, linked together by co-ordinating and
task-evaluation executive specialists in an organic
flux' (Bennis 1971, p. 550). What this means in

organisational terms is that there is no clear centre
and no fixed hierarchy. The centre is located
wherever the expertise is available to solve a problem,
and the head of the organisation is the individual able
to solve that problem at that time. When the problem
changes then so does the centre and the head. With
no clear centre there is no hierarchical pattern of
communication: communication is lateral rather than
vertical, consists of consultation rather than
command and contains information and advice rather
than instructions and decisions. Such an
organisational system can best be described by the
analogy of a net, each individual occupying the nodes
of the net and the communication patterns the
threads. Unlike a net there is a continual redefinition
of distances between nodes and a continual
redefinition of the relative importance of such nodes.
The normal is continual change and a continual
redefinition of tasks. The result of such change would
be instability on the structural level and insecurity for
the individual. The structural instability is countered
by a commitment to the objectives of the network,
e.g. in schools a commitment to education. In
Durkheim's terms a collective consciousness holds the
network together. The insecurity is met by individuals
rooting their social self in professional expertise.
Professional expertise derives its legitimacy from
outside the organisation and so provides a secure base
for the social self in a continuously shifting
organisation (a point made by Musgrove, 1973, when
he argued that subject specialists need to be retained
in schools), while at the same time such expertise is

valued by the organisation members as a resource available to solve the problems faced by them. (The above description of a feedback organisation is based on an amalgam of the ideas of Burns and Stalker 1961, and Schon 1973.)

The operation of such a feedback system in education is, Ben-David argues (Ben-David 1968), characteristic of higher education in the USA. It is characterised by a large number of autonomous and competing organisations whose internal structures are flexibly adjusted to meet the changing requirements of scientific collaboration. In contrast with this 'entrepreneurial system' the European system can be described as 'hierarchical'. It is often directly dependent on government, regulated by law and sometimes centrally controlled and directed. Internally the institutions of higher education are characterised by hierarchies of staff and hierarchies of research fields resulting in research being divided according to personal and institutional hierarchies rather than intrinsic interest or usefulness. A more detailed description of an educational organisation characterised by some aspects of a feedback organisation is provided by Richmond (1973). He describes Countesthorpe College as one in which there is, at least among the staff, a diminution of hierarchy. Decisions are taken by a moot of elected staff, and the head of the school (or the warden as he is called) does not retain the right of veto. Boundaries between subjects and between pupils are blurred and transcended with 'contextual areas' being studied by mixed ability groups. The objectives of the school are set out openly acting as a consensual ideology binding together the school as a unit.

This description of Countesthorpe demonstrates how limited has been the application of the egalitarian ideologies of deschooling and progressive education, and how one of the most revolutionary schools in the English state system still falls short of a feedback organisation. Arguments for schools to become feedback organisations demonstrate the implications of such a system of organisation in schools. Musgrove (1973) and Watts (1973) both argue for a less hierarchical relationship among staff. For Musgrove a feedback network has as its nodes subject specialists interacting with each other in diffuse networks. Such an organisational structure implies the demise of the head. He will become, in Musgrove's phrase, 'an archaic irrelevance' (Musgrove 1973, p. 11). Watts too implies the end of the head although he never follows up this implication (1973, p. 4):

the varied tasks facing the staff of a large school require . . . flexibility and adaptability on the part of the staff so that they may each undertake a range of roles . . . This requires . . . staff, including the head, to accept in one role a position of leadership, in another of participant, in another interpreter, in another supplicant, and so on.

The implications of this for the process of communication is seen clearly by the teachers involved to entail a continuous process of

consultation: 'Something far more complex than
"having a say in decision making". Essentially it is a
kind of self education. It therefore involves a
commitment to learning that is bound to entail pain
and struggle' (a teacher cited in Richardson 1974). As
Hamilton (1973) points out, such consultation must
involve all staff if bitterness is to be avoided and
co-operation achieved.

The implications of a feedback organisation for
pupils are illustrated by Armstrong (1973), a teacher
at Countesthorpe College. He argues that the pursuit
of truth requires that the role of teacher and pupil are
reversible. This means that pupils and teachers
together must plan the curricula. If this happens then
education becomes a 'collaborative exercise in
learning. . . in which each side recognises the special
position of the other' (p.53). To achieve this a
teacher is needed who can combine educational
guidance with intellectual leadership, but he argues
(p.57) that such a paragon is not available and
therefore the combination must be provided by a
group of teachers:

> I imagine a small group of teachers, three or four
> or five, working with a group of some hundred
> pupils, more or less. . . they are part pedagogue,
> part master, part fellow pupil, part interested
> spectator. . . In a society which respected the
> student's autonomy, such small co-operative cells
> would be at the centre of the educational process.

A feedback organisation in education would imply

therefore the abolition of hierarchies amongst staff
and between staff and pupils, a readiness on the part
of members of the organisation to continually
redefine their roles to meet new problems, and a
definition of education that saw it as a problem
solving operation. It would necessitate a
commitment by all those involved to some over-riding
objective and it would imply that the individuals in
the organisation had some secure social self
independent of the organisation. The reverse
statement also holds: if any of the egalitarian
ideologies are to succeed in education then the
organisational form most congruent with them would
be a feedback organisation.

What pressures are there within education for the
adoption of a feedback organisation, or elements of
it, and what forces of resistance are marshalled
against its introduction? Two groups of teachers
have organised themselves into pressure groups to try
and create non-hierarchical schools. The most radical
of the two is the Rank and File group within the
National Union of Teachers. They take as their
starting point the egalitarian ideology and see an
attack upon the inegalitarian structure of the school
as a way of attacking an inegalitarian society: 'The
school unit reflects in miniature the hierarchy of
outside society' (Rosenburg p.13). They therefore
argue for positive discrimination in favour of schools
in working class areas, free nursery education, the
abolition of public schools, the replacement of
competition by collective endeavour, the abolition of
exams and with respect to the school itself they

> seek a democratic system in which all aspects of
> school policy are decided by all who have a stake
> in the school — pupils, teachers, ancillary workers,
> parents and members of the outside community of
> workers; the Head and other officials to be elected
> by all members of the school community, and be
> subject to recall. All teachers to be paid a single
> salary scale (Rosenburg p.24).

The other group calling for a non-hierarchical school
takes as its starting point the professional ideology.
As Corwin (1965, p.313) points out:

> Professionalisation. . . is a drive for status. It
> represents the efforts of some members of a
> vocation to control their work. In order to
> monopolize a type of work, a vocation in the
> process of professionalization will seek to wrest
> power from those groups which traditionally have
> controlled the vocation.

This is precisely what a group of ILEA teachers are
proposing. In their pamphlet *The Right to Learn* (p.2)
they assert that 'teaching is the most important job in
a school'. This statement is underlined to emphasise
its importance. It follows a paragraph on the same
page in which they say:

> There are many teachers who feel they cannot
> play a full part in schools which have a hierarchical
> staff structure; this contributes to staff turnover.
> The increased division of functions within the
> school — administrative, organisational, pastoral,

social, teaching — has caused many teachers to feel
that they cannot fulfil themselves *professionally*,
or do a good job as far as the whole child is
concerned. The more senior the teacher's position,
the less actual teaching is done. (My emphasis.)

Their proposal is to set up a school with a
non-hierarchical structure of teaching staff: 'all
functions of the school administration will be shared
equally by all the teachers; executive power will be in
the hands of the whole staff' (p.2).

Those supporting deschooling are as small in
number as the supporters of the egalitarian ideology
or the professional ideology. In England the
deschoolers are closely connected with the radical
rejection of society that Musgrove (1973) calls the
'counter-culture'. The counter-culture has as its core
the immorality of boundaries and seeks to destroy
the conventional boundaries of morality, good taste
and normal perception. It is associated with drugs,
mysticism, pacifism and a rejection of authority. As
with the counter-culture, the rejection in the free
school is of authority and authority structures with a
concomitant celebration of spontaneity. The
Liverpool free school, for example, is a
non-hierarchical commune of teachers with no one
person in charge, no fixed curriculum for pupils, no
compulsion to attend lessons. The aim is to create a
sense of belonging — a community. In its lack of
hierarchy, its call for commitment to an ideology of
total acceptance of the Scotland Road area, it
resembles a feedback organisation. The description

one of its members gives of the role of members also
suggests a feedback organisation in that the role is
constantly changing and fluid: 'no one has just one
role. If someone arrives to join us they are not given
any specific duties. . . . Instead each person finds out
what needs to be done and what possibilities there
are and then goes ahead with whatever task he wants
to do' (Andrew Churchill cited in Richmond 1973,
p.173). In the USA deschooling has been more
rigorously pursued and the Parkway Program is a
literal expression of deschooling in that there is no
school. The city of Philadelphia forms the classroom.
Organisationally it is composed of cells of students, a
teacher and a university intern who meet four times a
week; ten cells combine to form a unit with its own
staff and headquarters and once a week the entire
population of the program meet to elect committees
to deal with the administrative and social tasks of the
program (see Richmond 1973). The students plan
their own course of study, within certain constraints
such as ensuring basic literacy, which involves them
not only with their teacher and his assistant but also
with local community agencies who supply tuition on
their own areas of expertise. The result fits Bennis's
description exactly: 'adaptive problem-solving,
temporary systems of diverse specialists, linked
together by co-ordinating and task-evaluation
executive specialists in an organic flux' (Bennis 1971,
p.550).

Much larger both in numbers and in institutional
support are those supporting the progressive ideology.
The ideology has become institutionalised in courses

in colleges of education throughout Britain and has
physical reality in primary education and in small
units such as the Centre for Applied Research in
Education, responsible for the Humanities Curriculum
Project, which was originally founded to propagate
progressive educational ideas. These supporters of the
progressive ideology couch their calls for change in
terms of curriculum reforms, but they have become
aware that to call for a change in curriculum is to
also call for a change in organisation. As Hamilton
(1973, p.154) says:

> the introduction of integrated studies is not merely
> equivalent to introducing a new syllabus but
> implies a radical change of emphasis in the
> organisational context and thinking of secondary
> education. . . simple questions of content cannot
> be separated from complex questions of grouping
> children by ability, from questions of
> 'responsibility' and authority, or even from
> questions of school democracy.

However against these pressure groups, against the
institutional support some ideologies have managed
to achieve and against the ideologies themselves are
marshalled very strong forces of resistance. The
concept of hierarchy is very deeply rooted in English
education. The abolition of hierarchy requires the
complete restructuring of secondary education in
terms of pupils, teachers and knowledge. This is
strongly resisted because, first, the social structure of
secondary education has created and maintains

conceptions of self and any attack upon that social structure will be seen as an attack upon that social self. This is particularly true of conceptions of self that are bound up with the hierarchy of knowledge. The teacher's own academic career before he begins teaching is a process during which he is progressively defined as, and comes to define himself as, a particular subject specialist. He sees himself as a historian or a geographer who happens to teach, not as a teacher who teaches history or geography (Kob 1961). An attack upon the academic hierarchy becomes therefore an attack upon the teacher's self-conception and will be bitterly resisted. Second, such an attack will be resisted because it will attack the present system of power and status from which the power and status holders gain great gratification. Teachers support hierarchies because they provide them with a career line. A teacher gains extra income and extra status from obtaining a graded post. The giving of a graded post also acts as a signal to the teacher that he is achieving something significant in a job which has few clear guides to who are the successful and who the failures. They support the hierarchy of teacher-pupil because without it their own efforts are belittled; if they are no more expert than the pupil, which is the implication of the open curriculum, then their own strivings to become expert in a subject are devalued. Unless they can gain new satisfaction from the role of 'resource manager for learning', i.e. unless they can concentrate upon their pedagogic rather than their academic position and gain status from that, then an open curriculum implies their own

efforts have been to little avail. Pupils as well as
teachers like a career line. They compete for the
status positions of monitor, class captain, prefect and
they want to know their exam marks and grades in
relation to others in their class. Like their teachers
they like structures that provide them with markers
so that they can measure their progress. Third, an
attack upon the present hierarchical structure of
secondary education will be resisted because it will
be seen as an attack upon the social order of the
wider society. Schools which replace competitiveness
with co-operation, abolish examinations and reduce
or eliminate hierarchy are in a disjunction with our
society. Our society, especially our economic system,
requires of schools (and universities) that they act as
sieves through which talent is shaken. A school that
does not act as a selection device would be flying in
the face of the real world outside its walls. To ask
that such schools be the norm rather than the
exception is to question the social order in our
society (a point recognised by J. Ford, 1969, when
she suggests a 'crammers' college' for the last two
years of schooling where pupils work for
examinations, leaving the rest of the school system
to concentrate on education rather than selection).
A school system that strove to inculcate co-operation
rather than competition — if it could be created
against the wishes of parents, employers, and pupils —
would of necessity lead to a re-appraisal of the
ordering of society. Finally there is strong resistance
because the attack upon the present social structure
comes from those who want to replace structure by

fluidity, boundaries by openness. Such an attack will
be seen not just as an attack upon our social order
but as an attack upon any social order and will be
labelled anarchistic and dangerous.

What are the possible responses then to a call for
open education? There are at least seven:

1 It can be ignored in the hope that it will go away.
  This has been the tactic that has been used by the
  ILEA when faced with those teachers who are
  calling for a new type of non-hierarchical school.
  The teachers' letters and visits have been met by
  officials stressing that their opinions have been
  noted.
2 A counter-attack can be launched. The Black
  Papers (Cox and Dyson 1969) constitute such a
  counter-attack: the traditional values are
  re-affirmed and the traditional structures
  supported.
3 It can be contained and isolated: open education
  can be limited to a few experimental schools or to
  a few departments in a school or it can be limited
  to specific age, sex or ability groups such as school
  leavers. This has the advantage of channelling the
  energies of the proponents away from the more
  radical attempts at implementation.
4 A purely nominalistic change can be made: the
  geography and history departments can be merged
  as the environmental studies department in which
  the old functions are carried on under a thin
  umbrella of co-ordination and a rhetoric espousing
  integrated education.

5 It can be classified as an interesting philosophical
   speculation which has nothing to do with the real
   job (the fate of this book?).
6 The people supporting it may be suppressed,
   dismissed or barred from positions from which
   they could implement open education by being
   promoted.
7 It can be implemented.

It can be seen from the preceding arguments that
implementation is most unlikely. Calls for its
implementation appear to occur at two points. First,
when the existing structure is under such strain that
it ceases to provide gratification to those working
within it. This appears to be the case for at least some
London teachers at the moment who faced with the
problems of inner city areas, lack of finance and large
classes (because many of their colleagues are 'voting
with their feet' to escape such problems) are calling
for a non-hierarchical school. Within the present
structure of secondary education it is at the point of
strain — created by the raising of the school leaving
age that many teachers are experimenting with some
form of open education. Second, calls for
implementation occur when a new structure is being
created in the formation of a comprehensive school.
Given a clean slate, its proponents argue, it is possible
to set up a less hierarchical school structure. This may
be possible with an entirely clean slate but our world
is historical and contains historical legacies of old
ideas, attitudes and problems. A study of the creation
of a comprehensive from a mixed grammar, a boys'

modern and a girls' modern (Easthope 1973) suggests
that these historical legacies are very important. The
merging of the schools was seen as an opportunity to
create a new type of education based on enquiry
methods. However the teachers in the new school
had been teachers in the old schools. They were used
to children of a limited ability range, and many had
only taught children of one sex. In the new school
they were being asked to teach children of all
abilities and both sexes. In addition they were
participating in a new school which had new
structures, both formal and informal, of power and
status. On top of this they were then asked to
abandon their authority as subject specialists and
teach using new methods of enquiry. The result was
'anomie' — a state of boundlessness. They had no
fixed reference points to attach themselves to in this
new situation. The response of the head and his
advisers was to re-impose subject boundaries very
firmly (these became the basic units of the school
structure with heads of subject departments having
special meetings and selected subject heads helping
to decide policy) and to introduce a fifty-two-page
booklet setting out in detail the duties of staff in the
school. Thus the old subject identity was re-asserted
and central control was re-asserted in the form of
bureaucratic guidelines and procedures. Whether this
would be the case in an entirely new school is
difficult to answer because there has been no
empirical research on such schools. However it would
seem likely that hierarchies would prevail given the
training and educational experience of all teachers

and also given the fact that a new school is usually started by appointing the head, which is the pivotal hierarchical position.

Even if open education is implemented in some form of feedback organisation despite the resistance to it and despite the obstacles derived from the past to its effective implementation, it will still face problems in itself. A feedback organisation requires a commitment from all its members and it requires problems upon which to focus. There is no reason to presuppose that all the members of a feedback organisation will share the same commitments. The John Adams High school in the USA is already faced with this problem: it has pupils who aren't committed to educating themselves and has as yet found no way to meet this problem (Richmond 1973). It may not only be a difference between pupils and teachers in terms of commitment however: teachers too may be expected to have differing levels of commitment and commitments to different objectives, which may not be solved by continuous feedback because they represent fundamental divisions of opinion. Does this imply a continuous process of schism in educational organisations with new educational sects continually forming? Similarly the organisational form presupposes an agreement on the problems upon which to focus. This agreement may also not be forthcoming. In short the feedback organisation is held together by agreement rather than power. In a programming organisation a diversity of views and objectives can co-exist as long as those holding them

do not challenge the power holders. In a feedback
organisation there must be agreement on objectives or
there is no longer an organisation. This necessity for
agreement creates further problems. Agreement and
even a limited consensus without being imposed by
the powerful require discussion and argument. Such
discussion is time-consuming. Unless the discussion is
itself seen as part of the education process (as a
'teach-in' may be seen) then it may be resented. It
also implies small numbers or some form of
representative democracy, for if all are to contribute
there can't be too many or not everyone will be able
to contribute. The creation of representative
democracies creates its own problems of delegates
versus representatives, long office for stability versus
short office to avoid oligarchy etc. (see Cohen, 1971,
for a discussion of this). Finally there is the problem
of self identity in a feedback organisation. There
seems little doubt that the constant change endemic
to such an organisation would create social insecurity
for the individual unless he had a self identity rooted
outside the organisation. This means for feedback
organisations in education a professional identity as a
teacher (identity as an academic would re-introduce
hierarchy) — a manager of learning resources. Such a
professional identity would require as much effort to
create and meet as much resistance as the creation of
a feedback organisation itself.

For supporters of the anti-hierarchical ideologies
my conclusions then are pessimistic. The
implementation of these ideologies requires a
non-hierarchical organisational structure and such a

structure seems unlikely to be created in the face of
resistance to it and even if it is adopted in a limited
form or in marginal areas of education then it will
raise many new problems.

Conclusion

An organisation that is congruent with conceptions of
open education has been postulated by theorists of
organisation, social theorists who see us moving
toward a post-industrial society and educationalists.
Such an organisation is best characterised as a process
rather than a structure. The organisation is a
constantly changing system, or network, of
communication. The focus is upon the system not
upon the units which comprise it because the units
are constantly being brought into and out of the
system and continually being redefined as the system
changes. Such an organisation has no clear centre, no
fixed categories and consequently no hierarchies and
it continually transcends boundaries. The cement that
holds together this organisational form is an
agreement by those involved in it upon the goals to
be achieved.

Some supporters of egalitarian ideologies
(specifically deschooling) and supporters of the
professional ideology have called for, attempted to
implement or are asking for resources to implement
organisations which in their lack of hierarchy
approximate the organisation described. They have
met and will meet strong resistance. Hierarchy is

deeply rooted in English education and a conception of the school as a 'hierarchical community' is more congruent with increasing bureaucratisation than less structure. Even if implemented where normal organisations fail or possibly in new schools, the organisational form carries with it problems of its own. It creates insecurity for individuals who are asked to work in a permanent state of 'anomie' or boundlessness. More fundamentally it creates problems of educational goals because it is held together by agreement on goals rather than structures of power. There is no reason to believe that such agreement will be achieved for all members of such an organisation and without such agreement there must be a re-assertion of structure or continual schism, with new educational sects forming around new educational prophets.

Bibliography

ABRAMSON, E., et al. (1958) 'Social power and commitment: a theoretical statement', *American Sociological Review*, vol.23.

ARMOR, D.J. (1973) 'Has busing succeeded?', *New Society*, 18 January.

ARMSTRONG, M. (1973) 'The role of the teacher', in *Education Without Schools*, ed. P. Buckman, Souvenir Press.

BALES, R.F. (1950) *Interaction Process Analysis*, Addison Wesley, Cambridge, Massachusetts.

BANKS, O. (1971) *The Sociology of Education*, Batsford.

BARNARD, C.I. (1938) *The Functions of the Executive*, Harvard University Press, Cambridge, Massachusetts.

BARON, G. (1955) 'The English notion of the school' unpublished paper, London Institute of Education.

BARON, G. (1970) 'Some aspects of the "headmaster tradition"', in *Sociology, History and Education*, ed. P.W. Musgrave, Methuen.

BATES, A.W. (1970) 'The administration of comprehensive schools', in *Comprehensive Education in Action*, ed. T.G. Monks, National Foundation for Educational Research.

BEN-DAVID, J. (1968) *Fundamental Research and the Universities*, OECD, Paris.

BEN-DAVID, J., and ZLOCZOWER, A. (1962) 'Universities and academic systems in modern societies', *Archives Européennes de sociologie*, vol.3.

BENNIS, W.G. (1971) 'The coming death of bureaucracy', in

Emerging Patterns of Administrative Accountability, ed.
L.H. Bowder, McCutchan, Berkeley, California.

BERNSTEIN, B. (1958) 'Some sociological determinants of
perception', *British Journal of Sociology*, vol. 9.

BERNSTEIN, B. (1967) 'Open schools, open society?', *New
Society*, 14 September.

BERNSTEIN, B. (1971) 'Education cannot compensate for
society', *New Society*, 26 February.

BERNSTEIN, B. (1971) 'On the classification and framing of
educational knowledge', in *Knowledge and Control*, ed.
M.F.D. Young, Collier-Macmillan.

BIERSTEDT, B. (1950) 'Analysis of social power', *American
Sociological Review*, vol. 15.

BLOOM, B.S. (1956-64) *Taxonomy of Educational Objectives*,
McKay, New York.

BOTTOMORE, T.B., and RUBEL, M., eds (1963) *Karl Marx*,
Penguin.

BUCKMAN, P., ed. (1973) *Education Without Schools*,
Souvenir Press.

BURNHAM, P.S. (1968) 'The deputy head', in *Headship in the
1970s*, ed. B. Allen, Blackwell.

BURNS, T. (1954) 'Directions of activity and communication
in a departmental executive group', *Human Relations*,
vol. 7.

BURNS, T., and STALKER, G.M. (1961) *The Management of
Innovation*, Tavistock.

COHEN, C. (1971) *Democracy*, Free Press, New York.

COHEN, L. (1970) 'School size and head teachers'
bureaucratic role conceptions', *Educational Review*, vol. 23.

COLEMAN, J.S. (1973) 'The concept of equality of
educational opportunity', in *Equality and City Schools*, eds
J. Rayner and J. Harden, Routledge & Kegan Paul.

·CONWAY, E.S. (1970) *Going Comprehensive: A Study of the
Administration of Comprehensive Schools*, Harrap.

CORWIN, R.G. (1965) 'Militant professionalism, initiative,
and compliance in public education', *Sociology of
Education*, Summer.

COX, C.B., and DYSON, A.E., eds (1969) *Fight for
Education*, Critical Quarterly Society.

CROWTHER REPORT (1960) *Fifteen to Eighteen*, HMSO.

DAHL, R.A. (1961) *Who Governs? Democracy and Power in*

an American City, Yale University Press, New Haven, Conn.

D'ANTONIO, W.B., and ERICKSON, E.C. (1962) 'The reputational technique as a measure of community power', *American Sociological Review*, vol. 27.

DONAGHY, T. (1971) 'Research into Ireland's comprehensives', *Comprehensive Education*, vol.18.

DOUGLAS, J.W.B. (1968) *The Home and the School*, MacGibbon & Kee.

DUMONT, L. (1972) *Homo Hierarchicus*, Paladin.

DURKHEIM, E. (1933 edn) *The Division of Labor in Society*, Free Press, Chicago.

DURKHEIM, E. (1961 edn) *Moral Education*, Free Press, New York.

EASTHOPE, G. (1973) 'Power, bureaucracy and community and their relation to size in secondary schools in England and Wales', unpublished Ph.D. thesis, University of Exeter.

ETZIONI, A. (1961) *A Comparative Analysis of Complex Organisations*, Free Press, New York.

FLOUD, J. et al. (1957) *Social Class and Educational Opportunity*, Heinemann.

FLOUD, J. and HALSEY, A.H. (1957) 'Intelligence tests, social class and selection for secondary schools', *British Journal of Sociology*, vol. 8.

FLOUD, J. and SCOTT, W. (1961) 'Recruitment to teaching', in *Education, Economy and Society*, eds A.H. Halsey, J. Floud and C.A. Anderson, Free Press, New York.

FORD, J. (1969) *Social Class and the Comprehensive School*, Routledge & Kegan Paul.

GIDDINGS, A. (1968) ' "Power" in the recent writings of Talcott Parsons', *Sociology*, vol. 2.

GLASER, B.G. (1963) 'Attraction, autonomy, and reciprocity in the scientist-supervisor relationship', *Administrative Science Quarterly*, vol. 8.

GOFFMAN, E. (1961) *Asylums*, Doubleday, New York.

GOFFMAN, E. (1963) *Behaviour in Public Places*, Free Press, New York.

GOLDHAMER, H., and SHILS, E. (1939) 'Types of power and status', *American Journal of Sociology*, vol. 45.

GOSS, M.E.W. (1961) 'Influence and authority among physicians in an outpatient clinic', *American Sociological Review*, vol. 26.

GRIFFITHS, A. (1971) *Secondary School Reorganization in England and Wales*, Routledge & Kegan Paul.

HAGE, J., AIKEN, M., and MARRETT, C.B. (1971) 'Organisation structure and communications', *American Sociological Review*, vol. 36.

HALSEY, A.H., ed. (1972) *Educational Priority*, vol. 1, HMSO.

HAMILTON, D. (1973) 'The integration of knowledge: practice and problems', *Journal of Curriculum Studies*, vol. 5, no. 2.

HARGREAVES, D. (1967) *Social Relations in a Secondary School*, Routledge & Kegan Paul.

HOBBES, T. (1962 edn) *Leviathan*, Fontana.

HOLLY, D. (1965) 'Profiting from a comprehensive school', *British Journal of Sociology*, vol. 16.

HOLLY, D. (1972) *Society, Schools and Humanity*, Paladin.

HOMANS, G. (1951) *The Human Group*, Routledge & Kegan Paul.

IAAM (Incorporated Association of Assistant Masters in Secondary Schools) (1960) *Teaching in Comprehensive Schools: A First Report*, Cambridge University Press.

ILEA (Inner London Education Authority) TEACHERS (undated) 'The right to learn', unpublished ms.

ILLICH, I.D. (1971) *Deschooling Society*, Calder and Boyars.

KATZ, D., and KAHN, R.L. (1966) *Social Psychology of Organisations*, Wiley.

KING, R.A. (1968) 'The head teacher and his authority', in *Headship in the 1970s*, ed. B. Allen, Blackwell.

KING, R.A. (1969a) *Education*, Longman.

KING, R.A. (1969b) *Values and Involvement in a Grammar School*, Routledge & Kegan Paul.

KING, R.A. (1971) 'Unequal access in education — sex and social class', *Social and Economic Administration*, vol. 5.

KING, R.A. (1973) *School Organisation and Pupil Involvement*, Routledge & Kegan Paul.

KING, R.A. (1974) 'Short-course neighbourhood comprehensive schools — an LEA case study', *Educational Review*, vol. 26.

KOB, J. (1961) 'Definition of the teacher's role', in *Education, Economy and Society*, eds A.H. Halsey, J. Floud and C.A. Anderson, Free Press, New York.

LACEY, C. (1970) *Hightown Grammar*, Manchester University Press.

LAMBERT, R., et al. (1968) *New Wine in Old Bottles*, Bell.

LIPPIT, R., et al. (1952) 'The dynamics of power', *Human Relations*, vol. 5.

LUNN, J.B. (1970) *Streaming in the Primary School*, National Foundation for Educational Research.

LYND, R.S., and LYND, H.M. (1929) *Middletown: A Study in Contemporary American Culture*, Harcourt Brace, New York.

MARCEAU, J. (1975) 'Education and social mobility in France', in *The Social Analysis of Class Structures*, ed. F. Parkin, Tavistock.

MAYS, J.B., et al. (1968) *School of Tomorrow*, Longman.

MECHANIC, D. (1962) 'Sources of power of lower participants in complex organisations', *Administrative Science Quarterly*, vol. 7.

MIDWINTER, E. (1972) *Priority Education*, Penguin.

MILES, M. (1968) *Comprehensive Schooling: Problems and Perspectives*, Longman.

MILLER, D. (1958) 'Industry, and community power structure: a comparative study of an English and American study', *American Sociological Review*, vol. 23.

MITCHELL, G.D. (1964) 'Education, ideology and social change in England', in *Explorations in Social Change*, eds G.K. Zollschan and W. Hirsch, Routledge & Kegan Paul.

MOORE, H. (1921) 'The comparative influence of majority and expert opinion', *American Journal of Psychology*, vol. 32.

MUSGROVE, F. (1973) 'Power and the integrated curriculum', *Journal of Curriculum Studies*, vol. 5.

NEWSOM REPORT (1963) *Half our Future*, HMSO.

PEDLEY, R. (1969) *The Comprehensive University*, Inaugural lecture given at the University of Exeter.

PERCIVAL, W. (1968) 'The head and the problem of size', in *Headship in the 1970s*, ed. B.Allen, Blackwell.

POSTER, C.D. (1971) *The School and the Community*, Macmillan.

RICHARDSON, E. (1974) *The Teacher, the School and the Task of Management*, Heinemann.

RICHMOND, W.K. (1973) *The Free School*, Methuen.

ROSENBURG, C. (undated) *Education and Society*, Rank and
    File Teachers.
ROSENTHAL, R., and JACOBSEN, L. (1968) *Pygmalion in
    the Classroom*, Holt, Rinehart, New York.
ROSS, J., et al. (1972) *A Critical Appraisal of Comprehensive
    Education*, National Foundation for Educational Research.
ROUSSEAU, J.J. (1968 edn) *The Social Contract*, Penguin.
ROUSSEAU, J.J. (1969 edn) *Émile*, Dent.
ROWE, A. (1969) 'The school counsellor from the
    headteacher's viewpoint — I', in *Guidance and Counselling
    in British Schools*, eds M. Craft and H. Lytton, Arnold.
SCHON, D.A. (1973) *Beyond the Stable State*, Penguin.
SCHOOLS COUNCIL (1970) *Sixth Form Survey*, HMSO.
SELLECK, R.J.W. (1972) *English Primary Education and the
    Progressives 1914-1939*, Routledge & Kegan Paul.
SHARMA, C.L. (1963) 'A comparative study of the processes
    of making and taking decisions within schools in the UK
    and the USA', unpublished Ph.D. thesis, University of
    London.
SHIPMAN, M. (1967) 'Education and college culture', *British
    Journal of Sociology*, vol. 18.
Statistics of Education for England and Wales (1972) HMSO.
STINCHCOMBE, A.L. (1968) *Constructing Social Theories*,
    Harcourt, Brace, New York.
SWIFT, D.F. (1966) 'Social class and achievement motivation',
    Educational Research, vol. 8.
SWIFT, D. (1973) 'Status systems and education', a course
    text in *Education, Economy and Politics*, Course E352,
    Open University.
TANNENBAUM, A.S. (1956) 'The concept of organisational
    control', *Journal of Social Issues*, vol. 12.
TANNENBAUM, A.S. (1961) 'Control and effectiveness in a
    voluntary organisation', *American Journal of Sociology*,
    vol. 67.
TANNENBAUM, A.S. (1962) 'Control in organisations:
    individual adjustment and organisational performance',
    Administrative Science Quarterly, vol. 7.
TAYLOR, G., and AYRES, N. (1969) *Born and Bred Unequal*,
    Longman.
TAYLOR, W. (1968) 'Training the head', in *Headship in the
    1970s*, ed. B. Allen, Blackwell.

TRAUB, R.E., et al. (1972) 'Closure on openness: describing and quantifying open education', *Interchange*, vol. 3.

TRONC, K.E. (1967) 'A conceptual model for the study of the communication of authority in a bureaucratic education system', *Journal of Educational Administration*, vol. 5.

TURNER, V.W. (1974) *The Ritual Process*, Penguin.

UNESCO (1971) 'Social background of students and their chance of success at school', *Educational Documentation and Information*, 45th year, no. 179, UNESCO, Paris.

VAUGHAN, M. (1969) 'The grandes écoles', in *Governing Élites*, ed. R. Wilkinson, Oxford University Press.

WALBERG, H.J., and THOMAS, J.C. (1972) 'Open education: an operational definition and validation in Great Britain and the United States', *American Education Research Journal*, vol. 9.

WALLER, W. (1932) *The Sociology of Teaching*, Wiley.

WATTS, J. (1973) 'Sweating out the conflicts', *Times Higher Educational Supplement*, 2 November.

WEBER, M. (1948 edn) *From Max Weber*, eds H.H. Gerth and C.W. Mills, Routledge & Kegan Paul.

WEBER, M. (1964 edn) *The Theory of Social and Economic Organization*, Free Press, New York.

WEINBERG, I. (1969) *The English Public Schools: The Sociology of Elite Education*, Atherton, New York.

WILKINSON, R.H. (1970) 'The gentleman ideal and the maintenance of a political élite', in *Sociology, History and Education*, ed. P.W. Musgrave, Methuen.

WILLENER, A. (1965) 'The worker and the organisational system', in *Workers' Attitudes to Technical Change*, ed. A. Touraine, OECD, Paris.

WILLIAMS, R.M. and FINCH, S. (1968) *Enquiry I: Young School Leavers*, HMSO.

WILSON, B. (1966) 'An approach to delinquency', *New Society*, vol. 7.

WISEMAN, S. (1967) 'The Manchester survey', Appendix 9 in *Children and their Primary Schools*, Plowden Report, HMSO.

YOUNG, M.F.D. (1971) 'An approach to the study of curricula as socially organized knowledge', in *Knowledge and Control*, ed. M.F.D. Young, Collier-Macmillan.